Mindfulness Training

How Mindfulness and Meditation Will Change Your Life and Kick Depression Away

(How To Be In The Present Moment In Your Everyday Life)

Brett Baker

Published by Rob Miles

© **Brett Baker**

All Rights Reserved

Mindfulness Training: How Mindfulness and Meditation Will Change Your Life and Kick Depression Away (How To Be In The Present Moment In Your Everyday Life)

ISBN 978-1-990084-13-3

All rights reserved. No part of this guide may be reproduced in any form without permission in writing from the publisher except in the case of brief quotations embodied in critical articles or reviews.

Legal & Disclaimer

The information contained in this book is not designed to replace or take the place of any form of medicine or professional medical advice. The information in this book has been provided for educational and entertainment purposes only.

The information contained in this book has been compiled from sources deemed reliable, and it is accurate to the best of the Author's knowledge; however, the Author cannot guarantee its accuracy and validity and cannot be held liable for any errors or omissions. Changes are periodically made to this book. You must consult your doctor or get professional medical advice before using any of the suggested remedies, techniques, or information in this book.

Upon using the information contained in this book, you agree to hold harmless the Author from and against any damages, costs, and expenses, including any legal fees potentially resulting from the application of any of the information provided by this guide. This disclaimer applies to any damages or injury caused by the use and application, whether directly or indirectly, of any advice or information presented, whether for breach of contract, tort, negligence, personal injury, criminal intent, or under any other cause of action.

You agree to accept all risks of using the information presented inside this book. You need to consult a professional medical practitioner in order to ensure you are both able and healthy enough to participate in this program.

Table of Contents

INTRODUCTION 1

CHAPTER 1: POSTURE 3

CHAPTER 2: MINDFUL BREATHING 8

CHAPTER 3: THE POWER OF MINDFULNESS 13

CHAPTER 4: AN INTRODUCTION TO BUDDHISM 26

CHAPTER 5: ANXIETY CAUSES AND SYMPTOMS 33

CHAPTER 6: BENEFITS OF MINDFULNESS 57

CHAPTER 7: BECOMING NON-ATTACHED 66

CHAPTER 8: ENOUGH IS ENOUGH, IT'S TIME FOR A CHANGE 73

CHAPTER 9: HOW AND WHY MINDFULNESS WORKS 77

CHAPTER 10: PRACTICING MINDFULNESS TECHNIQUES 100

CHAPTER 11: MEDITATION IN BUDDHISM 105

CHAPTER 12: PAST, PRESENT AND FUTURE 114

CHAPTER 13: UNDERSTANDING YOUR BRAIN – SOME BASIC PSYCHOLOGY 119

CHAPTER 15: SIDE NOTE 126

- CHAPTER 16: WE MEDITATE - IN THE SAME BREATH 129
- CHAPTER 17: STEPS TO MINDFULNESS MEDITATION 138
- CHAPTER 18: MINDFULNESS FOR A HAPPIER LIFE 158
- CHAPTER 19: BECOMING NON-ATTACHED 163
- CHAPTER 20: DECIDE WHICH PRACTICE IS RIGHT FOR YOU TODAY 170
- CHAPTER 21: WHAT IS MINDFULNESS? 174
- CONCLUSION 202

Introduction

This book contains proven steps and strategies on how to be in a constant state of happiness.

Allow yourself to achieve peace of mind and relaxation by discovering mindfulness as a life changing experience. Eliminate stress from your life and learn how to concentrate on the present, accepting things for what they really are and without any judgment.

Here Is A Preview Of What You'll Learn...

What does mindfulness mean

All about mindfulness meditation and how it can help you

Effective mindfulness exercises that will help you reach happiness

The benefits of mindfulness

Mindfulness uses

The impact mindfulness has on your mental and physical health

How to achieve peace of mind

How to let go of the past and unnecessary attachments to negative things

Obstacles to mindfulness and how to get over them

Much, much more!

Thanks again for downloading this book, I hope you enjoy it!

Chapter 1: Posture

While it might seem that meditation is something that only goes on in the mind—in reality, nothing could be further from the truth. Meditation should be understood as a process that involves both the mind and the body. Without employing the proper posture, your time spent meditating could be wasted.

If you were to travel the world and examine the hundreds of different meditation techniques out there, you would find their practitioners all appear one thing in common—they all employ a similar posture. This is not by accident. Virtually every meditation, from the most ancient to the most modern one, employs the same techniques to achieve a proper posture for meditation. This includes:

Sitting

Almost all meditation practices involve sitting. There are meditation pillows you can use to keep things comfortable. Variations on sitting include:

The Quarter Lotus: sitting with crossed legs and your feet beneath your knees.

The Half Lotus: sitting with crossed legs and one foot on top of the opposite thigh. The other rests beneath the opposite knee.

The Full Lotus: sitting with crossed legs, and both feet are placed on top of the opposite thigh.

Burmese Position: if you can't sit comfortably with your legs crossed, just sit however you feel comfortable—placing your feet on the floor.

The chair: if sitting on the floor is too uncomfortable, you can always use a chair; sit straight with your back away from the back of the chair and your feet firmly on the floor.

Elongate the Spine

Once you have a firm base in your seated position, straighten your spine so that an imaginary rod could go through the top of your head, down your spine, and directly out your bottom. Imagine your spine elongating as you sit so that you will feel uplifted while you are meditating. You can think of your spine as something made up of all vertebrae—like a slinky, stretching slightly towards the sky.

Resting Hands

Place your hands on your lap. This is the most natural and comfortable place to put them. This should help you achieve a proper sitting posture. For a more traditional meditation posture, place your right hand on top of your left and just barely touch your thumbs together.

Relax Your Shoulders

Let your back and shoulders relax. Make sure your shoulders are not hunched with the stress of your day. To make sure, you can even push your shoulders back slightly but only a little bit—too far, and you will introduce new stress, which is something we are trying to avoid.

Tucking Your Chin

Tuck your chin in but just a little. This should make you look down slightly from straight ahead. If you find you are looking at your lap, you've tucked too far. Remember—just a little.

Open the Jaw

This doesn't mean to open your mouth but to relax your jaw, allowing any stress in your face to dissipate. Lightly touch your tongue to the roof of your mouth so that you can breathe more easily. Make sure your teeth do not clench, as this will add stress and make it more difficult to meditate.

Rest Your Gaze

Look a few feet ahead of you at the floor. If your chin is in the correct position— when you look straight ahead, that is where your eyes will fall. Adjust your chin tuck, so looking directly ahead, rest your eyes two to four feet from where you are sitting. Meditate with your eyes open, to begin with. This will help you avoid the distractions that can come when you close your eyes, like images and daydreams, and it also helps keep you from falling asleep. A more experienced practitioner can meditate with eyes closed—but for now, keep your eyes open.

If you do find yourself falling asleep while you try to meditate, here is a solution brought to you through the ages by very wise practitioners of the ancient meditation schools: get more sleep!

Chapter Summary: remember the following points each time you prepare to meditate. They will set you up physically for success:

Sitting

Elongate the spine

Resting hands

Relax your shoulders

Tucking your chin

Opening the jaw

Rest your gaze

Chapter 2: Mindful Breathing

To start being mindful, the first thing you need to do is make mindful deep breathing part of your daily schedule

You can do everything you do during the day with mindfulness including your breathing. To succeed with other mindfulness meditation techniques, you need to master the art of mindful breathing. You can easily incorporate this deep breathing technique into your mindful meditation exercises.

Mindful Breathing 101

Mindful breathing is a simple mindful technique that has powerfully surprising results. The technique focuses on identifying your inhalations as inhalations and exhalations as exhalations. When you take in breaths, acknowledge that you are inhaling. When you breathe out, acknowledge that you are exhaling. It is that simple and that easy: **recognize every**

in-breath as an in-breath and every out-breath as out-breath.

However, you will never be able to achieve this without bringing your mind home to yourself and your present realities. Every mindful exercise has an object of focus, an anchor. It could be mindful eating, mindful walking, mindful dancing, or mindful talking. Here, the focus is on your breathing.

Here is what to do to make your mindful breathing count and help you attain a greater level of concentration and mindfulness:

Mindful breathing exercises require all the serenity and privacy you can get: because privacy and serenity ensures maximum concentration without interruptions.

Sit and relax in a very comfortable position and shut your eyes to keep away every form of visual distraction.

Place one hand on your chest and the other hand on your belly.

Breathe in deeply through your nostrils and tell yourself, "This is my in-breath." Breathe out through a half closed mouth and tell yourself, "This is my out-breath." Notice the hissing sound the air makes as it forces its way through your mouth.

The miracle of mindful breathing is that your mental discourse automatically terminates the moment you focus on your breathing. You need not force anything: it just takes a cue and everything goes silent in your head—no more thoughts about the past or worries about the future. No more thoughts about projects you have at hand. No thoughts about anything other than your breaths and the sensation they make as the air rushes in and out of your windpipe. With consistent practice, even when the thoughts appear, you can observe them nonjudgmentally and let them go just as fast as they come.

Take mindful breathing a step further by practicing gratitude. You can enjoy your breathing because you are alive. The dead do not breathe. You breathe because you are alive. Be mindful and thankful of this. Repeat the mantra, "I'm breathing, thus I'm alive." The greatest miracle is to be alive because only when you are alive can every other miracle become possible.

Enjoy the happiness that comes from celebrating the gift of life as brought to the fore by your mindful breathing sessions. Stay in that celebration mood for as long as you want (for the duration of your meditation sessions—you can start with as little as 2-minutes and then gradually increase the duration). Your in-breaths can be short or long. You must not try to lengthen or shorten it. Do not interfere with anything during this time. Your only task is to recognize your in-breaths and out-breaths and enjoy the feeling of happiness they bring as you relish the savory feeling of being alive.

Practice mindful breathing every day for 5-30 minutes (and if possible, two times a day). If you do this, you will start nurturing mindfulness in your daily life and activities:

Chapter 3: The Power Of Mindfulness

Mindfulness. It's a pretty powerful word. You hear it numerous of times in life and hear thousands more talking about how mindfulness improved their quality of life. To put it into perspective, mindfulness means that the mind is fully attending to what's happening now, to what you're doing and to the space you're moving through. This may seem unimportant, except for the maddening fact that we often lose sense with our bodies, we feel unmotivated, and pretty soon we are obsessed with the past and worrying about the future. And this only makes us anxious and nervous.

So, what is mindfulness and what can you do with it? In this chapter, we will learn the true extent of mindfulness and how it can change your life for the better. One definition is: Mindfulness is the basic human ability to be fully present to anyone, anywhere, at any time – it is being aware of where we are and what we are doing, and not overly responsive or overwhelmed by what's going on around us.

With the power of mindfulness, no matter how far you stray away, mindfulness is right there to clasp us back to where we are and what we're doing and feeling. If you want to harness the true power of mindfulness, it's best to practice it for a while. Mindfulness isn't something that you can apply spontaneously; it's something you apply gradually. Since it's hard to explain in words, you will find variations of its meanings and its extent through books, websites, audio, and videos. There's much to mindfulness, but it all boils down to awareness.

What is Mindfulness?

Simply put, mindfulness is the practice of living in the present moment. Mindfulness is a lifestyle change to better oneself. When you practice mindfulness, you practice living in a non-judgmental state of awareness of the present moment. Mindfulness does not dwell on the past or dreaming about the future. Instead, mindfulness allows you to focus on what is happening right now in the present moment.

Mindfulness revolves around Buddhism, in which it emphasized how important it was to live in the present moment. Mindfulness is about bringing your attention to what's happening right now rather than focusing on what you cannot control. Mindfulness comes with numerous of benefits that will be discussed in the following chapter. However, mindfulness is not meant as a change that can instantly improve your life. Instead, it is meant to be a change of lifestyle and attitude. You can perform mindfulness into all elements of your life, which means you will benefit from it more. However, even if you are only able to employ mindfulness in a few aspects of life, you will still reap the benefits. Being mindful will never be a mistake for you to try. Mindfulness is a change for the better. When you practice mindfulness, you practice genuineness, open-mindedness, forgiveness, and charity. You live from your heart and your soul. You do not allow your ego or social standards to control you. You are open, and you embrace yourself and what is around you. You look for the truth and learn from everything around you. You allow your atmosphere to teach you. Do everything that you do with a sense of purpose. You are responsive and proactive, so not reactive. You practice grace and accept your surroundings. Allow grace to teach you how to forgive and to love imperfections.

How Can Mindfulness Help with Stress?

You have probably heard that mindfulness helps reduce stress. But how does mindfulness actually help you do that? Well, the University of Oxford and the University of Massachusetts Medical

School strongly implies that mindfulness not only helps reduce stress but also lightly creates an internal strength so that future stressors have less influence on our happiness and physical well-beings. Here are some more ways on how mindfulness can help you cope with stress:

- With mindfulness, you become more aware of your thinking patterns. You then stop being so sensitive to your thoughts. This way, your stress response is not activated in the first place.
- You don't immediately react to a situation. Instead, you take a moment to pause and deliberate and then use your mind to come up with the best solutions and responses.
- Mindfulness helps make you more aware and sensitive to the needs of your body. You may notice pains earlier and can then take appropriate action to reduce or eliminate the pain, so it does not worsen.
- You are more aware of the other's emotions. As your emotional intelligence

increases, you are less likely to fall into conflict, in which in return, reduces the chances of stressful conflicts.

- Your level of care and empathy for yourself and others increases. This compassionate mind can help soothes you and inhibits your stress response.

- Mindfulness reduces activity in your amygdala. The amygdala is part of your brain and is central to activating on your stress response, so efficiently, your background level of stress is decreased.

- Mindfulness can better your focus. So, you can complete your work more efficiently, you have a greater sense of well-being, and this reduces your stress response.

- You can switch your attitude to stress. Instead of focusing on the negative aspects of feeling stressed, mindfulness offers you a new perspective on stress. You will think on how the increased pressure strengthens and energizes you to have a positive effect on your body, soul, and mind.

Benefits of Mindfulness

Mindfulness comes with a multitude of benefits. Some of these benefits will come from the simple understanding of mindfulness, and some benefits will come from additional work, focus, and dedication. It is best not to practice mindfulness to achieve these benefits, but to practice mindfulness just to live in the present, and allow the benefits to come your way. Here are some of the benefits come from mindfulness:

Mindfulness can improve your health.

Improving your health is always a beneficial thing! According to the American Heart Association, recent studies imply that meditation can help reduce blood pressure. One 2012 study of African-Americans with heart diseases showed that mindfulness meditation improves blood pressure. Focusing on the present is an excellent way to improve your future

health and current health. Here are some areas where mindfulness can help with your physical health:
- It can help relieve stress
- It can help treat diseases and cancers
- It can lower blood pressure
- It can reduce chronic pain
- It can improve sleep

Mindfulness can increase your focus.

One of our greatest challenges to getting things done is the distraction of the mind, while we try to get one job finished, our minds procrastinate and deviate away from our responsibilities. We check our social media and email hundreds of times of the day and eventually we never get things done. However, with mindfulness, it can combat all these distractions and brings you back to the present moment in order to get what needs to be done, done!

Mindfulness can help reduce your anxiety.

Anxiety can be crippling and far from fun and helpful. Anxiety can keep you from getting out of bed in the morning or taking on big tasks. Anxiety can severely hurt your social relationships and ruin opportunities. It has been proven that mindfulness can improve anxiety. It teaches you to focus on the current moment. You stop worrying about what others think of you or what others say about you. You concentrate on the present instead of dwelling on the past, and you stop worrying about the future. But, even if you do not have anxiety issues, mindfulness may help you through other aspects of life and solve other problems and may even improve your confidence.

Mindfulness can make you happier.

Happiness can be hard to achieve if you are not entirely concentrating at the present moment. Instead, you focus on the past and worry about what could have happened. If you are too focused on the future and what might happen, you cannot enjoy the present moment. Mindfulness can make you happier by encouraging you to live in the present moment. Enjoy the time that you have and the precious moments you have. Happiness can be reached by those who are mindful.

Mindfulness can help reduce depression and negative energy.

Sadness and depression can ruin your life. Many people have discovered that mindfulness can reduce depression and negative energy. When you practice mindfulness, you can take in those things that negatively affect you and change your environment accordingly. Stopping and slowing down can provide you the opportunity to identify your triggers to both deep depression and happiness. It can help you determine what areas you are happiest in and keep you there. However, mindfulness should not be your only solution to depression; it should take extra work and dedication to help you cope with it. Mindfulness with a combination of proper advice, assistance, and support may make all the differences in the world. It may help you reduce or eliminate your depression.

Mindfulness can help you find peace.

With mindfulness, it can help you find the peace that you did not know even existed. It is important that you feel peace flowing through you and that you enjoy this in the present moment. Peacefulness can make all the difference in life. If you are looking for peace, attempt mindfulness and you will notice a life changing improvement on your viewpoint towards life.

You appreciate things more.

Appreciation is a general result of practicing mindfulness. As you begin to pay more attention to your thoughts, you notice that you block us from appreciating the good things in life. Let's take for example when you get angry for getting stuck in traffic, if you align your focus to the current moment, you notice things such as the beautiful song on the radio or perhaps a child waving at you through another window. We can't feel grateful for things we don't notice, and so mindfulness and appreciation goes well together. When you become mindful of your surroundings and aware of life, you see the beauty we have never seen before. We see growth and transformation and changes where before we may not only have seen inactivity.

You learn the art of acceptance.

People spend a lot of time fighting with the present moment, rather than accepting it. Your thinking patterns are packed with thoughts like "I like this," and "I don't like that." We miss the joy of the present moment when we spend all our energy avoiding it. With mindfulness, we accept whatever is present and truly embrace it. It's all about acknowledging the moment we have right now. Then we can deliberate and decide if it's something we can change, we can then work in the next moment to change it. If it's not something we can change, at least we can prepare for the moment.

Mindfulness doesn't eliminate all the stressors from your life. Your children will still throw tantrums; people will still cut you off in traffic, you will still need to pay bills. It may seem that nothing changes, but yet everything changes! When you are mindful, you reduce stress, enhance your performance, gain insight and awareness by observing your mind, and increase your attention to other people. The thoughtful transformation that occurs takes place within you. You choose whether to eliminate the stressors in life more delicately. How does this change happen? Well, when you exercise mindfulness, you experience some pretty powerful insight and perspectives that lead to some pretty incredible shifts.

Chapter 4: An Introduction To Buddhism

Buddhism is a teaching that is prevalent globally and it is often described as a religion. However, there is a problem with that classification, as it tends to place Buddhism in the same frame of reference with other religions, especially the Abrahamic religions of Judaism, Christianity and Islam. Buddhism is remarkably different in what it teaches, how it teaches and how it is practiced. The reference to religion usually includes an element of faith and an element of worship. Those lines are blurred when you study the theme of Buddhism and when you delve deeper into the practices of the different strains of Buddhism that have emerged over the years.

Many forms of Buddhism have existed during various times since Gautama where Buddha first synthesized his wisdom into text. The four that have gained traction over time are Theravada, Mahayana, Vajrayana, and now, Zen.

Each strain offers a different dimension of the total teaching and interprets the teachings in a way, which resembles the collective consciousness of the followers. In the ancient interpretations, most notably in the Theravada texts, Buddhism is a teaching that shows us the path to enlightenment and nirvana.

Nirvana is a concept that emerges time and again in ancient religions and it does so in Buddha's teachings as well. Nirvana is said to be the end of rebirth, and it is the attainment of immortality, without the suffering, that characterizes the human condition.

At a fundamental level, most religions subscribe to the notion of good versus evil, saint versus demon, right versus wrong, and suffering versus bliss. In Buddhism, there is an element of this polarity as well, but it is presented in a different flavor, as we will see in the unfolding pages of this book.

The Spring of Buddhism

Buddhism began with the teachings Siddhartha Gautama. Siddhartha was the son of a local chieftain in a city within, what is now, Nepal. Siddhartha was born in the present city of Lumbini and was raised in the city of Kapilavastu. The actual year he was born is of historic uncertainty, but it seems to be circa 400 BCE.

It is said that Siddhartha was not allowed to look beyond his father's palace walls because of the suffering and poverty that prevailed amongst the lay people. His father did not want to depress or let young Siddhartha the agony of life's harsh reality and shielded him from the pedestrian life outside the palace walls. He married his cousin, Yasodhara at the age of 16, in an arranged marriage. They were both the same age. However, when he was older and did get a glimpse of the poverty outside the palace walls, he was bothered by it.

Before he turned 30, he gradually began to see the life beyond the palace walls. He was interested in getting to understand his realm and his subjects. Not having seen any of it within the palace walls, his exposure to poverty, death and disease, was significant. His chariot driver explained these concepts to him and the concepts shook him.

He decided to leave the palace and turn into an ascetic, where he renounced all possession and even relied on the kindness of strangers for his daily meals. His development continued to grow when he studied under the tutelage of two different yogis and succeeded to understand and practice deep meditation. This led to his ability to achieve high levels of meditative consciousness.

With that, Siddhartha attempted even deeper affinity with the universe by delving deeper into asceticism and fasting.

His initial attempt was to deprive the body of all worldly matter, but this attempt failed and it nearly cost him his life.

He decided to rethink his methods and turned towards a more spiritual path rather than a restrictive, physical path. In this realm, he turned to focus and concentration. No doubt, his experience with the yogic masters benefited his path to enlightenment.

Following an incident with a little girl who mistakenly thought him to be a spirit, Siddhartha sat under a Peepal tree - a **Ficus religiosa**, and vowed to remain until he reached his truth. He sat this way for 49 days in a state of mindful meditation and reached his enlightenment. He was said to be 35 years of age. From this point on, he was called the Buddha - in Sanskrit it means to be awakened.

The crux of his awakening is the knowledge he gained of what hunger, poverty, disease and death really meant. It was the answer to what he was seeking when he left his father's palace. Upon his awakening, he synthesized the experience into four truths - the Four Noble Truths, and these four truths are the pillars of Buddhism and inspire all its teachings.

With proper understanding of these truths, it is stated that a person can attain nirvana. That is the essence of Buddhism - to practice the four noble truths to attain nirvana.

The Four Noble Truths

The truths contained in the synthesis of Buddha's awakening are simple at first glance, but the ramifications can only be appreciated with practice and meditation. These four truths are:

that all things are unsatisfying when they are temporary;

continuously craving things that are unsatisfying;

stopping the craving and the clinging to unsatisfying things, will stop the cycle of rebirth; and, meditation and practicing mindfulness along with decent behavior and not being impulsive, will end the desire for all things unsatisfactory.

This was the beginning of Buddhism approximately 2500 years ago.

Over the course of history, civilizations and society's ways have changed gradually. Some of the teachings were not in direct harmony with some of the ways things were done and people continuously redefined many things. Different interpretations of the original Buddha teachings came into being. It took on different light and it advanced in some ways and regressed in others. For better or for worse, other teachings and principles entered the mainstream. As time passed, four main interpretations took on popularity. As mentioned earlier, the four are Theravada, Mahayana, Vajrayana, and Zen.

Chapter 5: Anxiety Causes And Symptoms

Anxiety can be quite an over bearing condition and one that can cause people to worry in excess. But to treat the disorder effectively, it is important for people to identify its triggers, and also understand its signs and symptoms.

Environmental causes

There can be several environmental triggers that can cause people to develop stress and, in turn, anxiety and some of the most prominent ones are mentioned here.

Pollution

Pollution is the number one environmental cause for people to develop anxiety. There can be a lot of chemicals in the air that can trigger off a stress response in a person. This pollution need not be vehicle emissions alone, and can also be factory smoke.

Crime

The rate of crime has increased by quite a bit, and living with the fear of being robbed or coming face to face with a criminal can cause people to develop anxiety. This is especially relevant in areas where crime is pretty rife.

Climate

Extremes in climate such as excess heat or too much cold can cause people anxiety. Their body will not be able to cope with the situation and their minds will start to produce excess cortisol.

Other Environmental causes include:

Stress from relationships - such as personal relationships, friendships, marriages not to mention the disasters that come with them such as separations, divorces

Trauma from events - Events include abuse, the death of a loved one or victimization that could come from events such as rape.

Stress from natural disasters – a tornado that wipes away your whole life, an earthquake that leads to the death of your entire family or a fire that burns up all your life's saving will indeed bring about anxiety in one's life.

Stress at work - It could be a nagging work mate, a rude boss or one that is constantly making passes at you.

Stress about finances and money – This can be so stressing more so when you have every eye on you yet things are not working out for you.

Change – While some people adapt to change so easily, some do not, and that is when anxiety can be developed. Small changes such as a new home, a new job and big changes such as divorce, death of a loved one can bring about anxiety when not received well. This is because change puts some people into a place where their emotions feel threatened due to unfamiliarity causing immense stress that culminates into an anxiety disorder.

Upbringing – Our lives are made up by a series of experiences and every one of these can do a lot in promoting or preventing one from suffering an anxiety disorder.

1.Children learn traits from their parents and so can they develop anxiety simply by watching how their parents react to situations. They also could learn anxiety from their parents' teachings.

2.Someone can also create social phobia because of some poor social reactions in their youthful years

3.One can also get fearful due to bullying or develop anxiety because he or she is worried about teachers, classmates or school in general.

Physical causes

Physical causes refer to the bodily problems that people might have. Some of these causes are as follows.

Illness

Illness such as cardio vascular or thyroid problems or stomach ailments can cause people to develop anxiety. They will start worrying about it in excess and this can cause them to be anxious.

Tumors

Tumors that can be present in the cerebral cortex of the brain can cause brain problems and also anxiety disorder.

PMS

Anxiety is a part of pre menstrual syndrome and girls who suffer from PMS can develop anxiety quite easily.

Hereditary

Although there is no conclusive evidence to prove that hereditary factors might cause people to develop anxiety, some researchers believe that there can be genetic modifications that can be passed on to children, and so, if the parents suffer from anxiety then the children might also develop it.

Biological Causes

Anxiety disorders can be caused by a number of biological factors such as:

Deregulation of brain chemical makeup – A number of studies show that an imbalance in one's brain chemistry will lead to anxiety. Research shows that people having anxiety disorders usually have problems with a number of brain chemicals or neurotransmitters such as norepinephrine, serotonin, as well as gamma-aminobutyric acid (GABA).

It has not been conclusively found out if these imbalances are as a result of poor copping strategies or if the imbalances come about first leading to one experiencing anxiety. The use of therapy that excludes any medication has been said to improve one's chemical regulation. This therefore shows that even though there is a biological component, the mind has the ability to overcome and improve neurotransmitters flow within the brain. Norepinephrine, serotonin, and gamma-aminobutyric acid are also crucial in emotional, mood, and sleep stability.

Genetics – Research has shown over and over again that some individuals are more prone to anxiety disorders than others genetically. Anxiety disorders seem to get passed on from parents and close family to children more so panic disorder.

However, it is not yet clearly known which genetic component is connected to upbringing but nonetheless, there is a genetic component involved. Therefore, people with close family relations that suffer from anxiety disorder should ensure that they reduce anxiety and stress in their lives.

Medical causes

There are some medical causes of anxiety and these include:

Though not so common, there might be some medical conditions that could lead to an increase in anxiety. These conditions include asthma, anemia, infections, and several heart conditions. This will occur when a disease or illness affects one's brain leading to a disruption in brain chemistry. In such instances, treating that condition will prevent any further anxiety.

Nonetheless, illnesses that lead to anxiety are not very common and anxiety can on its own make one to fear that he or she has these conditions even when not medically proven.

However, one can also develop stress due to a serious medical condition. This stress will in the long run lead to anxiety.

Anxiety can also be caused by lack of oxygen due to emphysema, a blood clot in the lung or pulmonary embolism

Use and abuse of Substance

Research has shown that almost half of the people using mental health services to treat anxiety disorders such as panic disorder, social phobia, panic disorder or GAD are using them because they are dependent on alcohol or benzodiazepine. In general terms, anxiety could also be as a result of:

Withdrawal from an illegal drug like heroin or from a prescribed drug like benzodiazepines, Vicodin or barbiturates

Intoxication from illegal drugs such as amphetamines, cocaine

Social causes

Social causes can be just as effective as environmental causes and there can be a few, which can be pretty potent.

Teasing

Being teased and bullied can give people immense anxiety. Whether at college, work or any other social place, being teased for looking a certain way or being of a particular caste etc. can cause people to develop anxiety disorders.

Influence

Social influence and peer pressure can also cause anxiety. Trying to be like others or trying hard to be recognized can cause people to undertake stress and develop anxiety.

Personal causes

Personal causes refer to personal issues that people might have in their family life.

Feuds

Family fights, misunderstandings etc. can cause people to develop anxiety. Living in a house where people are always fighting and bickering can greatly reduce the peace in their lives, and this can be quite taxing on people's minds.

Bad experience

Bad experiences such as abuse, rape, and molestation, especially occurring during early childhood can cause people to develop anxiety, and over the course of time it will only get worse and continue into adulthood.

Signs and symptoms of anxiety/ anxiety attack

Anxiety attack refers to a sudden emotional and mental attack that people can have at any time during the day and also during nights.

Panic

Panicking is one of the main symptoms of anxiety. Imagine a scenario that lasts for a couple of minutes followed by scary symptoms such as a pounding heart, weakness, tingling fingers, stomach pain, dizziness, and/or feeling hot. When faced with a stressful situation, people start to panic and lose their sense of focus. It will also cause them to worry in excess. In as much as not everyone who experiences panic attacks has an anxiety disorder, one that gets them repeatedly may be diagnosed with panic disorder. Such people are in constant fear about where, why and when the next attack may come about and tend to avoid places where previous attacks occurred. All in all, panic is a recipe for anxiety.

Insomnia

People with anxiety will stay up all night worrying about an issue and this will cause them to develop insomnia. While it might not be uncommon for someone to toss and turn when they have an interview or speech the next day, chronically staying awake through the night, agitated or worried about a particular problem or nothing specific is a sign that something is not right. Half of the people with general anxiety disorder (GAD) have sleep problems. Some other people with anxiety disorder may wake up feeling wired with their minds racing and they fail to find a way to calm down

Constant indigestion

While anxiety will always start in one's mind, it will often times be seen through physical signs such as constant problems with digestion. Such people will experience a condition called Irritable bowel syndrome (IBS) where one has cramping, constipation, bloating, stomachaches, gas, and/or diarrhea. It is basically the digestive system experiencing anxiety as well.

Although IBS will not always occur because of anxiety, these 2 conditions usually occur hand in hand and make each other worse. The digestive tract is very sensitive to psychological stress and likewise, social and physical discomforts caused by constant digestive problems make someone very anxious.

Irrational fears

Some anxiety is not general but it is linked to a particular scenario such as crowds, flying, or driving. If this fear gets to a point where it is disruptive, overwhelming and way out of proportion compared to the risk at hand, this is a sign that one has some phobia, which is a type of anxiety disorder.

While phobias can be damaging, they are not always obvious. They may actually never surface until one is confronted with a particular circumstance then he or she discovers that they are unable to overcome their fear. For example, someone who is afraid of frogs can go on for a long time without experiencing a problem, however, it is the moment that he or she comes face to face with a frog that they realize their need for help or treatment.

Stage fright

It is common for someone to feel butterflies before they make a speech or appear for any reason before a crowd. However, if the fear is so great to the point that no practice and coaching can help or if the person is always thinking and worried about it, the person might have a social anxiety disorder, also called a social phobia.

Patients of social anxiety usually worry for many days or weeks prior to a certain situation. Even when they manage to through with the event, they still stay very uncomfortable and dwell on it for a long time thereafter wondering how they faired or how they were judged.

Excessive worrying

Worrying a lot is one other symptom that shows that someone has anxiety or generalized anxiety disorder (GAD). However, what is 'a lot'?

If one has generalized anxiety disorder, a lot of worrying means having constant anxious thoughts on almost a daily basis for a period of 6 months. In addition to that, the anxiety is so bad that it interferes with one's day to day life and comes off with physical signs like fatigue.

When one has normal anxiety and another has an anxiety disorder, the difference will be seen from how bad their emotions affect them. If these emotions make one to suffer and become almost dysfunctional, then the person has an anxiety disorder according to Sally Winston, PsyD, co-director Anxiety and Stress Disorder Institute of Maryland in Towson.

Self-consciousness

Social anxiety disorder is not only seen when one has to address a big crowd, it could also be in day to day situations where one has to talk face to face with someone, or eat before a number of people.

In such scenarios, a person with social anxiety disorder will feel that everyone's eyes are trained on them causing them to blush, sweat profusely, have problems with talking or tremble. Such symptoms can be very disruptive and they make meeting new people, advancing in one's career, maintaining relationships very hard.

Tension in muscles

Someone who experiences constant tension in their muscles that is accompanied with general body muscle flexing, balling of fists, or clenching of the jaw, has an anxiety disorder. This sign is so pervasive and persistent that someone who has had it for a number of years may stop noticing it after sometime.

Indulging in regular exercises can help the tensed up muscles to ease up and to be kept under control. However, if an injury occurs or some unprecedented event that causes a disruption in the person's routine, the tension will flare up. Then all of a sudden they become a mess because there are unable to handle their anxiety in that state hence becoming irritable and restless.

Flashbacks

People that have posttraumatic stress disorder usually relive a traumatic or disturbing event, a violent attack or loss of a loved one. Some people with anxiety disorders also show these features or symptoms. Until recently, posttraumatic stress disorder was looked at as a type of anxiety disorder and not a condition all on its own.

However, flashbacks could occur in other anxiety types as well. A study published in the **Journal of Anxiety Disorders** of 2006 shows that some people that have social anxiety also experience posttraumatic stress disorder related flashback experiences. However, they may not be so traumatic, for example public ridicule. Such people usually avoid anything that reminds them of that experience – another symptom that is also experienced by people with posttraumatic stress disorder.

The need to be perfect

People with anxiety disorders have an obsessive and fussy mind set called perfectionism. If someone is always judging themselves or has tons of anticipatory anxiety regarding falling below their own standards or making mistakes, then that person has some form of anxiety disorder.

Perfectionism is also known as obsessive-compulsive disorder (OCD). Just like post traumatic stress disorder (PTSD); OCD has long been looked at as an anxiety disorder. Psychologists say that obsessive compulsive disorder could happen subtly, for example someone with OCD could take up to 3 hours applying makeup because for them it has to be just right and if any mistake is done, they start all over again.

Repetitive behavior

For one to be said to have obsessive-compulsive disorder, they must exhibit intrusive and obsessive thoughts that are coupled with repetitive or persistent behavior. This persistent behavior could be mental, where someone tells him or herself that all will be well time and time again, or it could be physical, where someone will indulge in something over and over again, say straightening things, washing hands.

This obsessive thinking and compulsive behavior becomes a fully blown disorder when the desire to complete the behaviors becomes the person's drive in life. These behaviors then become rituals to the person. For example, if a person has been adding 2 tea spoons of sugar into their cup of coffee and this one time, the sugar is used up hence can not make the 2 tea spoons, the person will get into total panic until they can put the usual 2 tea spoons.

Self doubt

Second guessing oneself or chronic self-doubt is a sign of an anxiety disorder.

People with generalized anxiety disorder and obsessive-compulsive disorder also experience this feature. Some times, this doubt could be about a question that is important to one's identity, such as, 'Do I love my children enough?'

Psychologists say that one will experience doubt attacks when that particular question goes unanswered. Patients of OCD believe, 'If only I would know 100% if I loved them enough or not, either answer would be fine,' however they are highly intolerant to uncertainty to the point that the question becomes as obsession.

Dry mouth

People suffering from an anxiety attack will start to have a dry mouth. Their body will be under so much stress, that their salivary glands will stop working and the mouth will start to go dry.

Chest heaviness

During an anxiety attack, the muscles that lie between the ribs start to expand and push against the ribs. This causes a heavy feeling to arise and makes people extremely uncomfortable.

Palpitations

Palpitations are a common side effect of anxiety. Palpitations refer to the heart beating unevenly or beating faster and deeper such that the person can feel their heart beating that way.

Headache

It is common for people with anxiety to develop a headache. This headache will not be the type that you develop during a cold and will be much sharper and spread all over the head.

Hyperventilation

Hyperventilation will mostly always occur during an anxiety attack. During hyperventilation, the person will start breathing deeply and end up eliminating all the oxygen from the body. This can cause them to experience breathing problems and feel like they are unable to complete their breath.

Limbs going cold

Limbs going cold are a common symptom. The fear and worry during an attack cause people's blood to not circulate properly and this will cause their limbs to go cold.

Limbs shaking

Limbs shaking can occur when the person is completely stressed out. Their hands and palms will start to vibrate and they will find it tough to hold anything properly.

Sweating

Sweating occurs when a person starts to panic. Sweating is a natural stress response to cool down the body and as the person will start to stress; their bodies begin to heat up.

Pale skin

Having regular anxiety attacks can cause people's skin to go pale and give them a sick look. Their skin will also start to dry out and their hair will turn brittle.

Sinking feeling

People start to experience a sinking feeling and wonder if it is the end of the world for them.

Feeling tired

People start to feel tired and incapable of thinking straight and doing anything that they must.

Feeling irritated

Feeling irritated and having a short fuse is quite common amongst people with anxiety disorder. The smallest of things can set them off and cause them to be angry and irritable.

Feeling confused/ irrational

Feeling confused about something and not being able to make a rational decision is also part of the signs and symptoms of anxiety.

Other symptoms could be:

- A feeling of going crazy or losing control
- Hot flashes or chills
- Trembling or shaking

These form the various signs and symptoms of anxiety and if you identify with these then it is best that you seek help.

Chapter 6: Benefits Of Mindfulness

Many traditions, both in the East and the West have practiced mindfulness for thousands of years. Fortunately, science is now confirming the benefits of these traditions. Science and scientists are trying to imbibe the qualities of mindfulness to affect our mental and physical well-being in a positive manner.

Mindfulness practices can be acquired through yoga, chanting, tai chi, mindfulness meditation, etc. These practices have proven to be good for your health. These practices help to illuminate the subjective world of our mind.

Mindfulness meditation has been derived from the Buddhist tradition. This stress reduction program has been proven scientifically to have an impact on the mindful awareness of our brain. It also helps us psychologically and brings about interpersonal changes. It can also positively affect our immune function.

The basic principles of mindfulness meditation have been also applied in a medical setting. It has been seen to help alleviate several medical conditions. The root of mindfulness is in the practice of focusing continuously for a long time. This can result in long-term changes in the brain. This is because the brain can change according to our response to an experience.

It may feel that mindfulness practice is simple but it may not necessarily be easy. to get the best results out of mindfulness, one needs to put in the effort and maintain discipline. It imperative because mindfulness forces us to go against the tide and break down our automaticity which has been forged over many years of our existence. Thus, a strong commitment and belief are required to practice the technique.

Therefore, it is imperative that

mindfulness practices should be carried out daily in a disciplined manner to see long-term improvements. Several leading institutions like the Harvard Medical School and the Massachusetts General Hospital are carrying out studies to prove the long-term effects of mindfulness practices.

It has been noticed that people practicing mindfulness develop an approach state in which they are more comfortable to face a challenge rather than to avoid it. This thought process creates a "left-shift" in the left frontal activity of the brain. Surprisingly this "left-shift" of the brain is also proportional to the positive changes in our immune system. This healing practice has helped HIV patients and also patients fighting psoriasis, by improving their immune system.

Mindfulness is good for our bodies and mind. Studies have proven that if one practices mindfulness even for a few weeks, one can bring about a lot of positive changes in oneself. Some of the benefits that have been proven by scientific findings are:

- Improvement in the immune system of patients with breast cancer and prostate cancer, after eight weeks of continuous therapy.
- Decrease in the usage of drugs and recidivism in a prison offering Vipassana meditation, and it helped to increase self-control and optimism in the inmates.
- Improvement in the physical well-being and emotional upliftment of students who received 15 weeks of counseling and therapy.
- Mindfulness can also bring changes to our brains. Practicing mindfulness increases the density of gray matter in the areas of the brain that is associated with memory, learning, regulation of emotion, etc.
- Mindfulness can also help us to increase our concentration and focus. It can help to reduce distractions and improve our

cognitive skills, memory, decision-making skills, etc.

- Mindfulness is also good for our minds. Half with the help of mindfulness therapy reduces the decrease in the recurrence of depressive behavior for patients. Mindfulness can increase positive emotions and helps to decrease negative emotions. So practicing mindfulness is a good alternative to taking antidepressants.
- Office workers noticed an 11% reduction in stress when they practiced mindfulness therapy for 20 minutes daily.
- A decrease in anxiety levels was observed by a group of researchers in the University of New Mexico.
- Mindfulness can also help nurture compassion in the person. When you practice mindfulness you are more likely to be benevolent towards your fellow human beings. Your brain is tuned to understanding the suffering around you and helps in regulating your emotions accordingly.

- Even teachers who receive mindfulness therapy are affected by less negative emotions, lower blood pressure, better compassion, which results in better and more effective teaching capabilities.
- Mindfulness also helps reduce Post Traumatic Stress Disorder (PTSD) amongst veterans.
- Mindfulness helps you to accept yourself as who you are. In this regard, it can help fight obesity. "Mindful eating" can result in eating healthy, savoring the food you eat, and in turn losing the excess weight. Even pregnant women can gain less weight and have healthier babies during their pregnancy.
- Practicing mindfulness can help you to build a stronger sense of self. It can help you to increase your self-esteem and make you more resilient to what people say about you. You will feel more beautiful no matter how you look. You need to love yourself first.

- Mindfulness therapy can help healthcare professionals manage their anxiety and stress better. It can also help improve their connection and empathy towards their patients by increasing the feelings of compassion towards their patients.
- Even teens can benefit from mindfulness therapy as it can help by reducing stress and depression.
- You can use mindfulness therapy to improve your business. Mindfulness can help you improve your focus, reduce stress, improve creativity, increase your positive energy which can help you to increase your confidence, resulting in better client satisfaction.
- Practicing mindfulness can help you become strong mentally and emotionally. Mindfulness training can be used by police officers, caregivers, veterans with PTSD disorder, etc.
- Practicing mindfulness can be rewarding for parents too. Research proves that practicing mindfulness can reduce stress

and depression in pregnant women and reduce development issues in babies. Even parents who practice mindfulness face lesser anxiety and stress. They emanate more positivity and in turn sustain better relationships with their children. It has been noted that less-stressed parents can deal better with their kids.

Mindfulness can help you to break free from the illusion of self. It can help you to embrace the moment that you are living in because that actual moment is life. As Tara Brach said, "What would it be like if I could accept life– accept this moment – exactly as it is?" Don't you want to find it out for yourself?

Chapter 7: Becoming Non-Attached

There's not a single good thing that comes out of developing attachments and if there's one, it is short-lived, as the negative side of attachments grows into us. Getting attached to someone or to something takes away your power, and more often than not, it ends up in a nasty experience. Let's say you are a young sweet woman with a bright future ahead. A prince charming comes along and sweeps your feet away. You are in love. Your world starts revolving around prince charming. It doesn't feel right when you go for a day without talking to them. When your prince charming is mad, you get mad, and when they are happy, you are happy too. It seems that your happiness is tied to their happiness. Then prince charming notices that you consider him to be a god among mortals. He starts despising you and his meager attempts to pull away inspires you to love him even harder. It is the sad classic tale of being attached to a person and it almost always ends in tears.

If you have been struggling with the negative habit of developing attachments, it's not easy to drop this habit. But there are mental training programs that would help us overcome this challenge. Mindfulness is one of the foolproof training that helps us to get rid of attachments and also equips us with a mindset that discourages getting attached in the first place.

The following are some of the ways that mindfulness allows us to fight against attachments.

No more getting wrapped up in fantasies

Nothing encourages us to get attached to something or to someone faster than a fantasy. When someone or something catches our fancy, we are quick to elevate them into a state of infallibility and what follows are vivid fantasies of what that person is like or how it would be so great to possess something. These fantasies hinder us from calling on the powers of our rational mind, and for that reason, we develop an attachment. Mindfulness empowers us to bring our focus to reality. Thus, our fantasies are banished away and now we have the mental clarity to see our situation for what it really is. The more we are able to think in a realistic way, the more we will behave in a well-adjusted manner, but if we are hanging on some fantasy, we are likely to exhibit strange behaviors.

Meeting your friends

Think about a young woman who has developed an unhealthy attachment to her boyfriend. She wants to spend all of her time with him and it doesn't matter whether he hurts her or not. She's blinded by her "love" for him. It would do such a woman a world of good if she tried to meet her friends. This is because our friends can be able to look at our situation through the lens of objectivity. Our friends can spot the inconsistency in our thinking and call us out on it. Furthermore, spending more time with your friends makes you realize that there are other important things needing your time besides your object of attachment.

Notice the disadvantages

It is not something that immediately occurs to us when we develop an attachment to something or someone. But noting down the disadvantages of this new development might awaken you from your negative habit. For instance, if you become attached to your spouse, so much that your whole days are spent thinking about them, they may have robbed you of time to check on your parents, do homework, and meet your clients. Ultimately, you will have to decide whether you can cope with these disadvantages.

Is this what we really want?

Call it desperation or what you may, but some of our behaviors are deeply unsettling. We could develop attachments as a way of coping with our inner battles and stay unaware. For instance, if we have been lonely for so long, we might become depressed about it. The next time we find a suitor or the next time someone shows interest in us, we will leap at them and plant our claws around them and declare them to be ours, never to let them go. The desperation can cause us to leap at virtually anything that moves. But in order to overcome this negative, we ought to ask ourselves whether what we have become attached to is something that we truly fancy. Taking a second hard look might jolt you awake from your crazy behavior.

Have a sense of fun

Instead of pursuing something and attaching yourself to it like glue, here's an approach that works. Have fun with it. Yes, you will spend time with the object of your interest, but the motivation will be different. You won't be looking upon this thing as the savior of your life, but you will be interested in knowing a little more about it. For instance, if you meet someone who is an absolute stunner, don't get their number and start text-bombing them with your declarations of your love for them. It's an obvious indication that you are fast getting attached, but even more than that, you pass off as creepy. Unless they are unstable too but expect that person to puff up their protective wings and try to distance them from you. But if you had approached them not as a needy person but as just a friend who's interested in knowing more about them, you will cover a lot more ground. They would let you into their life more easily. And getting to know what kind of person they truly are would probably kill the fantasy going on inside your mind and make you normal again.

Heal

The great thing about humans is that we have the capacity to know what's ailing us.

If we are suffering from unhealthy attachments, we can certainly research it and understand our problem. What remains is to take action so that we are no longer held prisoners of our negative habits. With enough commitment, we should get started and complete the journey to full recovery.

Chapter 8: Enough Is Enough, It's Time For A Change

For me, anxiety was always associated with discomfort in my chest. Many people have described anxiety as feeling abdominal stress, a burning sensation throughout their body, feeling short of breath and so on. No matter what your symptoms are I think we can agree that they are very unpleasant. So why should some people have to suffer from this while others don't? Why are they so lucky? Maybe you've found yourself dreaming of a life without having to be afraid of being embarrassed and making a fool out of yourself. Maybe you just wish that this feeling of being under pressure all the time could go away. Perhaps you're afraid of being alone. Whatever your fears are there is a way out I promise you that. Not all fear is bad of course but often time the fear that causes the anxiety is unrealistic.

So our goal is to decrease our fear and increase our feeling of being in control. But as you will find in the later chapters before we'll gain control, we have to lose it.

So the purpose of this chapter is to fuel you with enough reasons to want to change. So here are a couple of questions for you to consider:

• What are you missing out on because of your anxiety?

• What experiences could you be having right now if anxiety wasn't in your life?

• What relationships is your anxiety preventing you from having?

• How would you live your life if anxiety wasn't a part of you?

If these questions bring up a little bit of pain in you, then that's good. The biggest motivators in life are either pain or pleasure. Pain is the dominant one.

Here's an example: If I were to place 10 million dollars at the finish line, sure you're going to run fast to get it right? But let's say I place nothing at all at the finish line but a place a hungry wild wolf behind you who wants nothing more than to have a bite of you. In what situation are you going to run faster? I bet you chose the second one.

Understanding the fundamental idea behind motivation is crucial when overcoming anxiety. So as I mentioned, if these questions brought a little bit of pain, then that's good because that's going to propel you to want to keep going on your journey to overcoming anxiety. Now you might have some other questions that bring up, even more, pain in you and motivation to change. Use them to fuel you. It's time that you finally decide that enough is enough. "I can't go on living like this. There has to be more to life than this constant feeling of anxiety." Trust me, there is. I promise you that I will share all tips and tricks that have helped me to overcome anxiety. There is a wonderful life out there waiting for you. So let's find out how to get to the promise land shall we?

Key takeaways:

- Pain is the biggest motivator. Therefore, ask yourself painful questions like what am I missing out on because of my anxiety?
- Make the decision to change your life. Finally say enough is enough and commit to overcoming anxiety once and for all.

Chapter 9: How And Why Mindfulness Works

Imagine that you wade into a river and feel the water rush against you. You move up the river as you feel the water rush by you. You then move further down toward the end of the river, again you feel the water rush against you. It does not matter where you travel within the river, you feel water rush against you, and additionally it is the same water that is rushing against you, regardless of where you travel. The river is a metaphor for presence, also known as the present moment, or the Now.

No matter what we are doing, when we are doing it, or how we do it, all we are experiencing is the present moment; the present moment is eternal, there is no beginning or end. The experience of time, of a past, present, or future is just a construct of the mind; time is illusionary.

The perception of time, though illusionary, has profound implications on our experience of life. Fear is born out of the perception of time. Fear can only exist when anticipating the future. Further, fear is metabolized by the body. When fear and anxiety are ongoing, it breaks down the body. It is for this reason that people in war zones or other stressful environment seem to age at a faster rate than those not exposed to high levels of stress.

Mindfulness is about the quality of life, which is also related to the illusion of time. Our quality of life is sacrificed when we are distracted by fear, anxiety, or the illusions of time. How can we appreciate the profundity of life if we cannot even stay present long enough to enjoy the simple experience of taking a shower?

Slowing down the Mental Noise

Another benefit of mindfulness is the slowing down of the mental noise in our head, known as thought. Thought is truly a paradox as it is both all-powerful yet powerless. Thoughts are all-powerful because thoughts determine what we focus on, and they are the predecessor to action. Thoughts are powerless because they have no power of their own, all their power is derived from the attention that we give them. If our thoughts are of what is possible, or how to create value for ourselves and other, then this will be our experience of reality. If our thoughts are based on fear, we will make that our reality.

When we are consumed with thought, how can we connect with those we love, or make them feel valued? If we are consumed with thoughts, how can we experience the beauty of a sunset, the pleasure of taking a shower, or the appreciation for our own breath?

Mindfulness, Emotions, and Feelings

A lack of mindfulness is one the biggest reasons for the unhappiness of humanity. While engaging in thought, we are unable to be aware of the emotions and feelings that lie within us. We all have emotions or feelings that we try to avoid experiencing. In fact, the major reason for addictive behaviors, violence, guilt, resentment, and aggression are due to our efforts to suppress the expression of those emotions and feelings that we find painful. The problem is that emotions and feelings are energy forms, and just as small children, if they feel they are not getting the attention they desire, they will find ways to express themselves in other ways, such as those just mentioned. Our emotions are the overriding factor in determining the choices we make, even rational thinking cannot beat out the power of emotions. Our emotions, especially those that are subconscious, will override rational thinking if we are not aware of them. Just as with thoughts, emotions within themselves are powerless. They are only as powerful as the amount of attention we give them, or when we suppress them. To become mindful of your emotions and feelings, as you would to a guest, will allow your emotions to function in a manner that supports you in your wellbeing.

Nature of the mind

Before we discuss how and why mindfulness works, we need to discuss the nature of the mind. Imagine that you are in a theater watching a movie. This movie is full of drama, suspense, action, and comedy. You lose awareness to everything that is happening around you; you are totally absorbed by the movie. With each passing scene, you experience a shift in emotion. During the movie, you experience anticipation, concern, fear, anger, happiness, sadness, laughter, and suspense. Your state of being is as though it was on a roller coaster ride as each scene elicits a change in emotion or feeling.

Now imagine this situation, you are watching the same movie, and you are enjoying all the range of thoughts, feelings, and emotions that come from experiencing it; however, you are also fully aware of what is happening around you in the theater. You are aware that it is just a movie and do not get caught up in it. The movie may elicit a wide range of emotions from you; yet, a sense of peace or calm remains with you. You enjoy your movie experience fully, while never forgetting it is just a movie.

These two scenarios are a metaphor for life. You are the one that is watching the movie, while the movie is your mind. The first scenario represents the lives of most of us. We are totally absorbed in our thoughts, memories, beliefs, and perceptions, all of which contribute to the shaping of our sense of identity and our experience of life. Without exception, all of our problems and sufferings, individually or collectively, arise because we are absorbed with our mind; we are absorbed in the movie.

Can You Relate?

Rob wakes up Monday morning at 7:00 a.m. and goes for his morning jog. As he is running, he witnesses the beauty and calm of the morning. His sense of well-being is relaxed and calm. Upon returning home, he takes a stumble and sprains his ankle. Now Rob is feeling upset and frustrated; he is in pain.

Because of the accident, he is running late for work, making him anxious as he needs to attend an important meeting. He calls work to advise that he will be late. Rob's manager tells him not to worry as the meeting was canceled. Now Rob experiences a sense of relief. Rob arrives at work when he is informed that his boss wants to speak to him; Rob is now worried. Rob meets with his boss, who tells him that he is receiving a promotion. Rob is now feeling excited and very happy. At the end of the day, Rob drives home but winds up in a minor traffic accident; a car rear ends his new vehicle. Rob is now irate. This scenario illustrates how Rob's state of being is constantly changing, based on the situations and events that he experiences. In the course of one day, Rob went from relaxed, calm, upset, frustrated, anxious, relieved, worried, excited, happy, and irate. There is nothing wrong with experiencing these emotions; our emotions are what make us human. Problems happen when we allow our emotions to determine our state of wellbeing or our sense of identity.

Rob's state of well-being and his sense of identity were being determined by the situations and events that he encountered. Most of us are like this; we allow the ever-changing circumstances of our lives to determine how we feel about ourselves and the world around us. We are like the person in the movie theater who is totally absorbed in the movie. We also experience a roller coaster ride of thoughts, emotions, and feelings; we forget it is just a movie.

There is another way to live, one where our state of happiness and well-being is not determined by our situations or circumstances, nor is it affected by our thoughts and emotions. When in this state of life, our sense of well-being is based solely on the wisdom and understanding of whom we are at deeper levels of our being. To become enlightened is to understand ourselves at a level that is beyond experiences and appearances.

Time Traveling

When we think of enlightenment or an enlightened being, we may think of a guru or a wise sage. We may believe that enlightenment is reserved for the few and that it takes a great amount of time and practice to achieve it. In truth, none of these beliefs are true. You do not have to develop enlightenment, nor do you have to find it. Enlightenment is found within every human being. The potentiality or seed for enlightenment is within you already. You always had it, and you always will. Even when you pass away, your enlightenment continues. The problem is not that you do not have enlightenment; the problem is that you do not realize it. The reason you do not realize it is because you experience illusions of the mind; you are caught-up in the movie within your mind.   The purpose of developing mindfulness is to see through these illusions so that your enlightenment can be experienced and known by you. Greg wakes up in the morning and gets ready for work. Even before getting out of bed, he is thinking of his agenda for the day. He thinks of what he needs to do when he arrives at work. While taking a shower, Greg thinks about the emotional conversation that he had with his girlfriend the other day. He also thinks about the fact that he still needs to select a gift for his parent's anniversary. Greg gets into his car and drives to work, all the time thinking of how much he would like to take time off to go camping. Greg arrives at work, and for the entire day, he thinks about the next upcoming meeting, the phone calls that he needs to return, and the decisions he needs to make to make his department more profitable. At the end of the day, Greg sits down and watches a movie. Though he is enjoying the movie, his mind intermittently drifts off as he thinks about the issues that are concerning him. He continues to think about these things when he retires to bed, only to cease his thinking when he finally falls asleep.

Greg represents the vast majority of humanity in that he lives his life through the time machine known as thought. Most of our thoughts have to do with the past (which we call memory) or the future (which we call anticipation). It is these two thoughts that consume most of our lives at the expense of being present or mindful. When we experience the past or the future, we are unable to experience the present, which does not get caught up in time. From a Buddhist perspective, time is just another illusion of the mind as there is only presence; we can only experience memory and anticipation in the present moment. So what is the present or present moment? It is awareness. Awareness is always constant. Thoughts, perceptions, sensations, and experiences are always changing; however, awareness is non-changing. In other words, you are the present moment. You are a presence, not as your mind or physical body, but as your awareness.

Self-Identification with the Mind and Body
Are you aware of your thoughts? Are you aware of the sensations of your body? Are you aware of your perceptions? Are you aware of your body? If you answered "yes" to all these questions, then who are you? If you are aware of all these things, then you cannot be them. Most of us base our sense of identity on our minds and bodies.

If we are worried, worry permeates our entire being. If we are sad, our being becomes sadness. If we are in love, that is what we experience. Because we identify ourselves with our minds and bodies, we experience ourselves as a separate self, which is why you do not confuse your sense of self with this eBook. Because you identify yourself with your mind and physical body, you experience a sense of separateness from those around you, but this is an illusion as well. During deep sleep, you have no sense of self or experience. In deep sleep, you experience pure consciousness, unlike during REM sleep when you experience dreams. As mentioned before, your essential being is awareness. As awareness, you have no experiences during deep sleep, even of yourself. Deep sleep is characterized by the awareness that is devoid of thought. Because there is an absence of thought, there is also no sense of identification. It is from this pure place that awareness is projected. We experience dreams because awareness is being projected on to our subconscious thoughts. When we awake in the morning, awareness is projected on to what we call "the world" or "reality." We experience the world because we believe that we are a separate mind and body. In fact, what we call the "the world" is just another projection. Who you are, at your most fundamental level, is awareness experiencing itself as various forms during the dreaming and waking state. All sufferings arise from attachment to our desires. There is nothing wrong with desire or the pursuit of it; desire is both natural and necessary. Nor is it wrong to feel disappointed for not achieving what we want or victorious for achieving our dream. Our thoughts and emotions are just part of life; they are forms of energy that we experience. The difference between feeling like a success or a failure in life has nothing to do with the thoughts and emotions that we experience; rather, it is our relationship that we have with them that makes the difference. When we identify with our thoughts and emotions, our sense of self will constantly fluctuate as thoughts and emotions change. When we are experiencing positive thoughts, we may say to ourselves or others "I am feeling good." If we experience a setback or concern, we may say to ourselves "I am worried" or "I failed." Any thought or word that follows "I" can become an aspect of our identity, if we believe it. The following is an example of identifying with our mind:

A person who is angry walks into a room where there is a dog. The dog responds to the person by keeping its distance. If there are people in the room, they may keep their distance as well. The resulting actions of those in the room will, in turn, have an effect on how the person experiences the situation. The person may be indifferent to the dog and feel undesirable that others people are not engaging him in conversation. On another occasion, this same person walks into the room feeling peaceful. The dog approaches him, wanting to be petted, which brings about a sense of affection from the person. People in the room start engaging this person in conversation, and soon he may be part of a group that is enjoying a good time. The person now feels accepted and connected with those around him.

With either scenario, the outcome of this person's experience had nothing to do with the room, the people in it, or the dog. In fact, it had nothing to do with feeling undesirable or peacefulness. What made the difference was how this person experienced himself. In the first scenario, the person experienced himself as an indifferent and undesirable person, while in the second scenario; the person experienced himself as an affectionate or peaceful person.

The person who is established in mindfulness would not tell themselves "I am an undesirable person" or "I am a peaceful person." Rather than identifying with the feeling, this person would be thinking "The feeling of being undesirable is arising" or "The feeling of peacefulness is arising." Buddhism teaches us that we are not our thoughts, emotions, or other mental functions; rather, we are the witness of these mental functions as they arise within us. To demonstrate this, do this exercise:

Sit or lie down and close your eyes. Allow yourself to relax.

Enhance your relaxation by placing your attention on the flow of your breath. Breathing normally, place your attention on the flow of your breath as you inhale, and the flow of your breath as it leaves your body during exhalation.

As you relax further, visualize a beautiful sunset. Visualize it with as much detail as possible. Note: Everyone visualizes, though this ability varies from person to person. Some people can see their visualizations in vivid detail, while the visualizations of others can be very vague or faint. This does not matter. Just make your visualization as real as possible according to your ability.

Now visualize a black cat, see it as vividly as possible.

Lastly, visualize a full moon. Again, make it as real as possible.

Now open your eyes.

During this visualization exercise, you visualized a beautiful sunset, a black cat, and a full moon. At no time did you confuse yourself for any of these visualizations. You knew that you were not the sunset, the black cat, or the full moon; you were the observer of these things. These visualizations were just thoughts that took on a visual dimension. Unlike the person in the proceeding scenario, you did not identify with these thoughts. The reason for this is that these thoughts were not considered as being important by your mind, so there was no self-identification with them. On the other hand, the person in the room scenario placed importance on his thoughts. Because of this, he took on the qualities of his thoughts; he became indifferent, undesirable, affectionate, and peacefulness.

Who are you?

If we are not our thoughts or emotions, then who are we? What is the nature of the self? Buddhism believes that our true nature is that which is non-changing and eternal. Imagine a house of mirrors as seen in carnivals and circuses. Upon stepping into the house of mirrors, you find reflections of yourself throughout the room. Intellectually, you know that what you are experiencing is the numerous reflections of yourself created by the walls of mirrors that make up the room. Upon leaving the house of mirrors, you find yourself in what you experience as the "real world," where numerous people, objects, and landscapes surround you. All of these things are seen as being other than you. There is never confusion that what you experience in your daily life is something that is separate from you. This kind of perspective is what most of humanity experience in their daily lives. In Buddhist philosophy, the house of mirrors is the accurate representation of reality. What we commonly refer to as the world, our environment, or our surroundings, is really a mirror reflecting our inner world. Ultimately, mindfulness is about developing the recognition that everything that exists arises from consciousness. The predominant belief among humanity is that we are physical being that is conscious of the world around us. Further, we believe that we are separate beings from the world around us. From a mind that is cultivated in mindfulness, there is only consciousness and that consciousness expresses itself as the mind, the functions of the mind, the body, and the universe itself. In fact, you are the universe; you are not in the universe, the universe is within you. You are a consciousness that experiences all of life, including that which you call you. Again, think of deep sleep. There is no experience in deep sleep because consciousness is not interacting with thought. What happens to you in deep sleep? Where do you go? You have no experience or memory of deep sleep, yet you know that you have been there when you wake up. Nothing can exist if there is no awareness of it. This awareness is pure consciousness from which all of the experiences arise, including that which you believe to be you. To experience this is to understand the "oneness" or "unity" of life.

Creating Reality

We can never know true reality as everything that we experience is a projection of our own minds. To illustrate this, let us use snakes as an example.

When you see a snake (or anything for that matter), information or data about the snake is taken in by your eyes. This information is then broken down by the optic nerve, which turns the information or data into electrical impulses. When these electrical impulses reach the brain, it converts the electrical impulses into an image. This image is enhanced by the information received by the other senses (touch, sound, smell, and taste), which are processed in the same way as sight, though through their respective sensory organs. Linguistically, we apply the label of "snake" to this image, based on the language that we know. Not only do we assign a name to this image, but we also assign meaning to it, which is based on our past experience or past learning. All of these steps work together to create our experience of "snake." Since everyone processes information differently, that which is called "snake" creates a different experience for each person. For most people, "snake" means something that you avoid, fear, or find distasteful. For others, "snake" is a source of fascination, admiration, and even affection; it all depends on how the information is processed.

Regardless of how we experience our mental representation of "snake," we never experience the ultimate reality of a snake. Everything that we experience is a projection of our own minds. We are not in the world; the world is within us. Even that which you refer to as "you," is just another projection of your mind. What is commonly referred to as "I" or "me" is a thought of which you have a very strong sense of identification with and have cultivated since the day you were born. The common spiritual adage "We are spiritual beings having a human experience" is completely accurate. When you can understand what has been stated in this paragraph on an experiential

level, not intellectually, your experience of yourself, others, and the world will take on a dramatic shift. You will go through life with a sense of equanimity, wisdom, compassion, and happiness that is most rare. Because all things in life are connected, your state of life will affect other people in a manner that supports their happiness as well as yours. The fundamental reason for the practice of mindfulness
is to relieve suffering and create happiness in this world. To practice mindfulness means, to be a scientist of your own being. It means to become quiet and still for the purpose of observing the mental functions of your mind so that you can take charge of it, rather than allow your mind to be in charge of you.

Chapter 10: Practicing Mindfulness Techniques

Eat mindfully. Mindful eating may even help you to lose weight by helping you to slow down and really enjoy your food.[9] You can practice mindful eating with a piece of fruit, such as an apple.

Hold the apple and look at it, observing the form, texture, or any writing that may be on it.

Feel the apple in your hands, or perhaps against your lips.

Bring it closer to your face and spend a few breaths smelling it. Notice if your body responds, such as salivating or increased desire to taste it.

Finally, take a bite of the apple, noticing how it tastes, what it feels like, and if it's enjoyable to chew it.

Practice mindful walking. You can also meditate while walking. Try taking a walk and as you walk, pay attention to the way it feels to walk, feeling your muscles move, bend, and stretch. Slow your pace so you can focus on your movements and the sensation of your feet touching and leaving the ground.

Doing a walking meditation barefoot can heighten the experience and allow you to feel many more sensations such as the texture and the temperature of the ground.

Focus on sensations. You can do sensation mindfulness meditation if you are experiencing pain or you want to tune in to your body. The skill can help reduce pain and tension in your body. Choose a part of your body to focus on, either internally or externally. Are sensations pleasant, unpleasant, or neutral? You can note "there is now a pleasant feeling" or "there is an ache here". Observe how the mind and body interact with these feelings.

A similar method that applies to both first two body-focused foundations is a form of body scanning; namely, scanning the body up and down to examine sensations and

then letting them go to pass onto another part of the body, or watching energy flow.
Instead of tuning out much of what surrounds you, tune in to each sense. Open your eyes and take in your surroundings, noticing any movement, colors, or objects that stand out to you. Notice any smells in the air. Notice any sounds, perhaps the hum of electricity, cars outside your window, or birds singing.
Make daily tasks a meditation. Anything can be a meditation if you do it mindfully. You can brush your teeth mindfully by tasting the toothpaste, feeling the bristles of the toothbrush, and feel the motion of your hand. Take a shower mindfully and notice all the ways you take care of your body during this time. Even driving to work can be a meditation: notice how you feel in the car, the way your body conforms to the seat, and observe the thoughts and emotions that you experience when confronted with traffic, and desired or undesired outcomes.

Whenever you do a mindfulness practice, remember the most important part is being present. Come back to your breath and observe your thoughts and feelings without following them or judging them.

Chapter 11: Meditation In Buddhism

Buddhism puts forward three major schools of thought that determine how you meditate.

The first one is the Hinayana School, which is seen as the "lesser vehicle." It is found in Asia; the information is written for the most part in Pali, the language spoken at the time of the Buddha. It aims to bring clarification to individual trainers.

The Mahayana School, which is regarded as the "greater vehicle," is found primarily in Japan and the larger part of Tibet. Its content is primarily written in the Sanskrit language. Mahayana aims to enlighten all human beings.

The third class, called the Vajrayana School, commonly referred to as the "indestructible vehicle," gives you the most mysterious practices of the Buddha. Another prominent school of Buddhist thought is known as Zen Buddhism, which is a subset of the Mahayana School. It tries to disclose the truth by destroying the illusions that tend to be fortified by our predictable ideas and philosophies that in turn, control our expectations, perceptions as well as responses. It gives you an exceptional type of meditation called koan, a mystery with no obvious answer to the enigma.

Although the Buddhist religion is most closely associated with meditation practice, all major religions have a form of this contemplative practice.

Meditation in Christianity

In Christianity, meditation is referred to as Centering Prayer. Early Christian meditators were called Desert Fathers. They prayed or chanted their practice. Now, all sects of Christianity have established meditation practices, as well as Catholic, Orthodox, Baptist, Lutheran, Quaker, Episcopalian, Shaker, and more.

In Islam, meditation practice is entrenched in the Koran and the knowledge of the prophet Mohammed. Islam's spiritual path called Sufism also has commentary from knowledge from a broad array of customs including the Hermetics, Zoroastrian as well as Pythagoreans. It is made strong by a well-established practice that puts in focus poems, parables, and other figurative forms of storytelling.

Meditation Practice in Hinduism

For many years, meditation has played a large role in every aspect of Indian religious life, to larger or smaller degrees depending on many aspects such as the individual, the chosen path and the stage of life. The word "Hindu" stands for India.

It's a country backed by a rich history of many traditions and rituals, plus the practice of Buddhism. Hinduism cannot be related to just one or a single context.

Instead, it bases on various texts such as the Upanishads, The Bhagavad-Gita, a treatise on the Nature of the God-head, the sagas of The Ramayana, teaching regarding man's duty to the world, and The Mahabharata.

Meditation as Practiced in Judaism

The term Qabalah refers to both to reveal and to receive. Qabalah refers to both a doctrine of the metaphysical and also to philosophy; this practice within which the custom of Qabalah refers to a symbolic code that is meant to help the practitioner to grow.

Learners of the Qabalah convert their inner Nature using external Nature. They then internalize the symbols then steadily absorb their characteristics via meditation practice. The Cosmo gram is the main sign of Qabalah.

The Tree of Life, comprised of spheres that are eleven in total, also called the sephiroth. Of the 11 spheres, one is hidden. The 11 spheres are interconnected by a total of twenty-two pathways.

A single sphere is called the Sephira, and each represents the various characteristics of the divine.

Each sephira has a different God-name, representing different characteristics of the divine:

Wisdom
The Crown
Knowledge
Understanding
Mercy
Severity
Victory
Beauty
Foundation
Glory
Kingdom

Each sign is related to a sephira, including the name, title, color, image, and a certain number. Meditation helps bring up the superior faculties of the individual, going past reason, consequently bringing the cipher to life.

Meditation Practices in Other Religions

Various spiritual practices have traditions that are nearly alike in function and form. They also offer various other techniques.

The similarity is usually a matter of degree or opinion. The discussion of how the various meditations practices are similar or different can be helpful to you depending on what you are after. This is why you need to begin from a more traditional definition of meditation.

Additionally, the states of mind that have been affected by chemical compounds such as drugs and other concoctions can be identical in various other ways thought they could be slightly different in other areas.

Meditation won't result in a loss of control or self-awareness. It is all about making your mind clear and your thoughts so that you can get to a better level as a human being.

Meditation can take on a number of forms, though each form uses the principles that are found in all the systems. Meditation makes use of the whole being, including your mind, body, and emotion. All these are taken into consideration to make sure you develop the right kind of awareness, transformation, and insight.

It seems it is a human need and desire to understand, or at least be alright with, the fact that we exist on this temporal plane. Human life, all sentient life, is filled with countless dangers and fears. The dangers are often outside us in the physical world: car accidents, floods, earthquakes, and volcanoes, just to name a handful. But, the fears, those come from within, so we need to travel within ourselves to discover how these fears take hold of us.

They can imprison us in a way that inhibits the ability to experience true happiness or bliss. Happiness can only exist within us; we can't truly find happiness outside ourselves, in the forms of things or even other people.

American culture has built an economic model constructed on the notion that we can obtain things, whether physically or metaphorically, that will provide happiness.

Simply put, meditation is the skill of being with ourselves, without any distractions, including our own thoughts and judgments. It is a practice, a continual one. No one is successful immediately. Remove that idea; it will liberate you. It's extremely important to remember and realize there is a specific formula to perform the right meditation; everyone has his or her own way of doing things.

Be gentle with yourself. Remember also that there is no "good" or "bad" meditation session. There is only mediation. Those adjectives we add onto our experience are just that, words. They are merely mental judgments that often change over time.

As S.N. Goenka of Burma, a meditation instructor who has taught thousands of people repeatedly says during his Vipassana guided meditation practices, "Start again!" This implies there is no beginning nor ending to meditation. It's not time to start this practice from some arbitrary beginning; it's merely time to start meditating again.

Chapter 12: Past, Present And Future

It is extremely important that you learn something from the above quotation by Kahlil Gibran. What he is saying is that people can only teach those willing to learn and that a good teacher leads you to looking inward for solutions. Mindfulness amounts to the same thing.

Imagine your brain being the size of a shoe box. Into that mind, you put all of your memories, all your emotions, your thoughts, your past, your dreams for the future and your present moment. There is so much in that box that it's hard for new, fresh thoughts to find space to grow. The problem that people encounter in their day to day lives is that their minds are filled up with clutter. Let's look at it from another perspective, because this is the perspective of mindfulness.

Past

The past is gone. It is what you have already spent. It is never going to come back. Of course, there will be times when you learn from past experience and that's not denied. What you need to be aware of is that in mindfulness practice, you have no room for regrets, past hurts and past failures because these negative influences stop you from actually being in the moment in which you now find yourself.

If your mind is too busy allowing itself to see the world in retrospect, it doesn't have time for now. Another moment passes and another opportunity to be at peace with yourself is gone. Therefore, your mindfulness should be aware that past isn't now. It's somewhere else. You cannot spend your mind power in thoughts of the past during your meditative practice and need to learn to let go.

Present

This present moment, the one where you read the words from this page is all that you have for now. No one on earth knows where their lives are leading, but they do know that now is very real indeed. Mindfulness makes you very aware of yourself in this space in time and that helps you to look at your bodily needs, your attitude toward life and the way your body and mind work. If you feel sadness in this moment in time because of a past hurt, you are not making the most of this moment. This is the crux of the matter. It's the moment to smell the roses. It's the moment to feel the sunshine on your face or to appreciate the raindrops on the garden. This moment leaves no room for thoughts that are fleeting either into the past or into the future.

Future

Of course you can have dreams. Everyone should have dreams or ambitions about what they want to do with their lives, but when you practice mindfulness, it concentrates on now. You are much more likely to reach your dreams by making the moment that you are in count for something.

It may be working toward something that you want to happen. It may simply be making arrangements to meet someone tomorrow, but see it in perspective. It hasn't happened yet. It is only a hope or a dream in this moment in time. Thus, the majority of your thoughts need to be centered in the now, which leads you to fulfilling your wishes, rather than being lost on thoughts of what might be.

Mindfulness as it applies to the future, present and past

People who argue that you cannot meditate with something on your mind are wrong. You can. However, when you practice mindfulness meditation, you cannot allow worries, dreams, thoughts of the past or fears for the future get in the way of your meditation. Your meditation fills your mind with peace in this moment and that takes care of the rest all on its own.

Mindfulness should become a way of life, savoring every sensation that your body experiences, savoring every experience as if it's a new one and being very aware of your body, your surrounds and everything that happens in each moment you pass. Wasting time on regret, anger and other negative emotions causes you more hurt long term and the vicious circle of negativity can follow you into the next moment. Therefore, you need to learn a new way of thinking that enjoys everything that the moment offers.

Chapter 13: Understanding Your Brain – Some Basic Psychology

What most of us aren't aware of, is just how much of a slave we typically are to our biology – and especially when it comes to neuroscience.

We have the illusion of self-control. That is to say that we feel like we choose what we do and we choose how we feel. If we're angry, it's be-cause of some injustice – we've thought about the situation and decided that anger is the correct response. If you're happy, it's because all is well with the world and you're content.

We then take all this information and decide what we want to do next and how we're going to perform at that activity.

But the reality is that we are not in charge of our brains. Rather, our brains are in charge of us. And they're largely controlled by our bodies and our situations too. Unless we understand the workings of our brain and we're able to take conscious control over the processes that dictate our moods, our motivations and more, then we are destined to remain at the whim of certain chemicals – and completely oblivious to that fact.

Who Are You?

Okay, so let's go deep right off the bat. Who are 'you'? What makes you, you?

The answer is your brain to a large extent. And your brain in turn is made up of billions of neurons – small cells that have tendril-like extensions reaching out and into the different corners of your skull. These neurons can be created, destroyed or changed via our experiences and they represent all kinds of things including memories, sights, smells, thoughts and 'commands' to move our body.

When an electrical impulse moves through a neuron, this means it is 'firing' and thus we experience whatever correlates with that firing. If you open up someone's skull and use an electrode to stimulate individual neurons, then one might make someone see a point of red light, one might make some-one move their arm and another might make them remember their Mother.

These neurons are all interconnected and the more often two neurons fire at once, the more connected they become. Thus, when one neurons fires, it is likely that others around it will fire depending on the strength of the firing (called an 'action potential), other activity in the area and the strength of the connection. Some 'clusters' of neurons form the major brain structures like the occipital lobe, motor cortex or hippocampus which are responsible for particular behaviors. Other neurons reach from one end of the brain all the way to the other!

Already you can see how your brain is not always entirely under your control. If you see something specific, then this will cause certain neurons to fire based on your memories and understanding of that object. But it might also cause surrounding neurons to fire, depending on the associations you've formed during that life-time.

And when certain neurons fire, they cause particular emotions. That's because neurons communicate across synapses – small gaps between the end of one neuron (the axon – which is like a tail) and the dendrites (like arms) of another.

At the end of each axon is the synaptic knob, which is filled with chemicals called neurotransmitters, held inside 'neuro vesicles'. When the synapse fires, it causes these neurotransmitters to be released and that then alters the behavior of the transmission and the surrounding cells. Some neurotransmitters are 'excitatory' and make other neurons more likely to fire. Others are 'inhibitory' and make them less likely to fire – and more sup-pressed.

Others have more complex roles. Some for example will make you more likely to remember something, while others will make you feel happy or sad. This is what controls the way you 'feel' about certain experiences.

Neurotransmitters are linked closely with hormones too. Some hormones act like neurotransmitters while some neurotransmitters can act like hormones. Essentially, hormones are longer lasting and generally produced in the body, while neurotransmitters have shorter-lasting effects and are produced in the brain. Even hormones produced in the body though are largely triggered by the pituitary gland, which is located in the brain.

See a lion for instance and your brain will sit up and take notice owing to the associations you form with that image. Relevant neurons will fire and because those neurons are coded with danger, they will release a number of neurotransmitters like dopamine and cortisol to increase activity and say that something important is happening. This increased activity causes more of the brain to light up and areas around the hypothalamus will then begin to trigger activity in the pituitary gland, producing adrenocorticotropic hormone. The adrenal gland will also be triggered at this point, releasing the hormone epinephrine, which is essentially a form of adrenaline. This is then what causes changes in the sympathetic nervous system.

This triggers physiological changes, including:

- The acceleration of the heart and lungs
- Vasoconstriction (thinning of the blood vessels)
- Dilation of the blood vessels leading to muscles
- Dilation of the pupils
- Inhibition of erection
- Sense of dread/anxiety
- Tunnel vision
- Thickening of the blood to encourage clotting after injury
- Pain reduction

- Contraction of the muscles
- Shaking
- Suppression of digestion and immune function

Essentially, the body now directs all blood, oxygen, nutrients and resources to the muscles and the brain, in order to aid in combat, escape or other physical activity.

All this is involuntary and all of this is controlled entirely by automatic responses throughout your body. And it completely changes the way you now think and the way your body operates. It changes the way people see you and it drastically effects the way you perceive everything that happens subsequently.

But it's not just during times of high stress that you see such uncontrolled changes throughout your body. And there are many complex interactions of chemicals and hormones going on inside your body all the time…

Chapter 15: Side Note

This is a good time to insert a few points that you should take note of as you continue into a state of mediation.

Up to this point, you have been building your ability to dive deeper into your mindful state. Only practice will expand your ability, so keep doing this without expectation of when it will bear fruit.

By paying attention to your breath, you have created a new skill of explicitly looking at the here and now. You have been only looking at your breath to the point it leaves your person, then you stop and look at the air that enters your person. It is the very definition of mindfulness and the very purpose of your conscious mind. You are placing what is happening to you here and now in the palm of your consciousness. By doing this, you are now telling your consciousness to handle just that. When you do that, the conscious mind becomes quiet.

Silence does two things. It brings peace and it brings acceptance. This peace is something that you can physically feel as it feels like the descent of something external. That is probably some of the ancients described it as a spirit entering your body. That serves well as an analogy. However, the peace that descends is just the release of the pressures placed on the consciousness when we revert its use to the here and now.

The silence that follows, then allows your consciousness to be open to instructions. These instructions come from your subconscious. These instructions from your subconscious are instructions that have been precisely calculated and any action that flow from this will be the best possible action you can perform.

The silence of your consciousness, in the absence of chaos, allows it to listen to the instructions it needs to get the body to do what it has to. Remember earlier on in this book, we talked about being the conduit between abstract and reality. Mindfulness sprouts a state of silence that allows the conduit to be clear of blockages and listen to what is being communicated from the subconscious (which is connected to the universe across all space and time) to the conscious (which is connected to just one point in space and time - here and now). Now, back to the steps.

Chapter 16: We Meditate - In The Same Breath

We hurry, fuss, eat on the move, stand in traffic jams, work, listen to reports, prepare speeches and give reports, go to visit friends, study - long and tedious seminars and lectures, our days - the cycle of life in life. In the confusion of days, you often want to be in harmony with yourself, to feel your own center, stability, and inner peace. Meditation is the means that will give us all this.

As studies show, the result of the practice of meditation becomes: an improved ability to concentrate; improving the quality of decisions; improving the ability to listen to others; improving our leadership skills; increased stress resistance; emotional maturity; and, most importantly, a state of mental balance.

But, let's say, a willful decision was made to start such a useful practice, to go beyond the limits of ordinary pleasant things. And how?

They say you need to buy a special bench, a set of incense, special music, read books, watch an educational video, then sit down and sit. And not just sit, but twenty minutes! I'm sure you've heard, probably, such?!

At a minimum, you may have a feeling of bewilderment: "How can we sit these twenty minutes in the chaos of daily fuss, in the confusion of the constant cares of our mind, in the midst of affairs and duties, desires, aspirations, and anxieties?" We sit down and ... The usual "noise." The flow of thoughts, everything ends with the fact that we get up and ... no longer sit down.

Many of us face this problem. We can look for solutions, ask "knowledgeable people" how to meditate, how to cope with a constantly distracted mind. But we will only be told we must sit, endure, read mantras, do yoga. We can follow the advice and sit, endure, read, practice, and then understand. This is no longer the case. It makes no sense to engage in that does not bring any pleasure, because it gives rise to a new conflict, which leads to even greater tension.

Such an approach could have worked a hundred, two hundred, perhaps even five years ago when the world was different, and people were different just as their minds were different. Everything was much slower, easier. Meditation techniques of that time were created, taking into account the conditions of that time.

Today, when our perception exists within the framework of 140 characters on Twitter. When our actions and decisions need to be kept within the minimum period of time. When the settings of our minds are completely different, a completely different approach is also required. Dedicating these twenty, ten, or even two minutes to meditation is almost impossible. We have changed; it is neither good nor bad; it is just a fact that must be accepted.

Such a technique is required that will be as simple as possible, as clear as possible, as convenient as possible, and "wearable-with-it." Such as to start right away, right here and now. Without forcing yourself, without exerting mental fists to the whiteness of mental knuckles.

At the same time, such a technique is necessary so that as we deepen into practice and develop new skills, we can easily continue our development and growth.

The good news is that such a technique exists. It is called accordingly: Technique "One Breath."

Technique

This technique is most suitable for "beginners," but it also contains everything necessary for the "veterans" of meditation. That is, it helps practitioners to take a fresh look at the practice for a long time, and also provides an easy and elegant way to make the practice deeper and closer to reality.

So, what is "One Breath" and how to practice it?

You would need to:

- forget about time - no need to keep track of time;
- forget about benches and music, incense, and other miscellaneous things — none of this is necessary;
- Forget about mantras, techniques, poses, other details - at this stage. We will not need any of this.

You also need to:

- close your eyes;
- take a deep breath, feel as much as possible the path of air through the nostrils to the lungs and then to the lower abdomen;
- note the moment of cessation of breathing;
- make a calm, soft exhale as much as possible after feeling the path of air back

from the abdomen to the lungs and further to the outside.

That is everything. Nothing more to do. It is enough to take one inhale, and then one exhale, that is, one cycle of breathing. The whole difference compared to the normal breathing process is that we consciously pay attention to the breathing cycle. We try to be aware of all the details of inhalation and exhalation, noting the smallest details of changes in the body.

When we breathe in, we realize how air enters the nose, how it moves into the lungs, how the lungs fill, how the diaphragm moves, how the chest cell expands, how the shoulders and stomach move.

Then at least in detail, we present the reverse movement. Observe the compression of the abdomen, the air outlet, the contraction of the diaphragm, the compression of the chest, the air outlet through the nostrils.

Such a detailed process does not leave us the opportunity to be distracted, as every moment something happens, and a new object appears for observation. This is the very essence of meditation. This is a living process; it is not constant; it constantly gives something new; every moment is unique, unlike the previous one. This is life itself.

But the main charm of this technology is its duration. It is very short. One cycle, everyone can realize without problems. The mind will not escape thoughts into anything else. We will not worry about time, problems, or what needs to be done. We just do not have time to go into it. This is the whole trick.

Let's start with this one single breath.

Totally aware of its course.

This is only "One breath," no more.

One, not a set of breaths for ten or twenty minutes.

One breath can be done right now!

One inhale and exhale what always happens and to which we rarely pay attention.

In the course of each day, in the hectic, it is easy for us to find one random moment for "One Breath." After some time, we will easily find another moment for one more when it will be convenient for us. And then another.

"The journey of a thousand miles begins with the first step" - it seems that this is how the Chinese comrade Lao Tzu used to say it. Any process of meditation, like any other action in our life, begins with breathing. Life itself begins with breathing, right?

"One breath" can be done immediately after waking up - there is nothing better for the inclusion of consciousness in a new day. "One breath" can be done before breakfast, lunch, any snack. "One breath" is easy to do before starting work, turning on the computer, going outside, completing the workday, answering a phone call, answering an e-mail message, SMS, on social networks. "One breath" can be done during negotiations, standing in a queue, before answering a question, at meetings and discussions - whenever you like, for breathing is always there, and we only pay attention to it, returning to reality over and over again.

It is easy to invite work colleagues to do "One Breath" together before a meeting or other group discussion. It is in order to come at the present moment, leaving everything that is not needed outside.

"One breath" happens here-and-now, at this very moment, in the only existing time, in the present. Breathe in? Fine. Exhale.

Chapter 17: Steps To Mindfulness Meditation

Today, mindfulness meditation is becoming more and more popular in different parts of the world. Based on research over the last 10 years, mindfulness meditation can provide numerous health benefits both to the mind and the body. In fact, scientists discovered that it helps in lowering high levels of blood pressure, relieving stress, and lowering the risk of cardiovascular problems, including heart disease. Mindfulness meditation also aids in improving mental health, strengthening the immune system, and slowing the process of aging.

On the other hand, there are still several misconceptions about mindfulness meditation as discussed in Chapter 3. Beginners in the practice find it difficult to get started and stay committed. The benefits would not be realized unless an individual knows the proper techniques of carrying out of mindfulness meditation.

The primary purpose of mindfulness meditation is to allow an individual to develop mindfulness or awareness in order to understand reality's true nature. Once an individual develops awareness, he is able to see how his thoughts and actions affect his life. In addition, an individual is able to establish better decisions, which lead toward greater harmony and peace within himself and his relationships.

There is a set of steps that one can follow in order to carry out mindfulness meditation correctly. This set is considered as a unique approach to discovering the true value of mindfulness meditation. These steps will guide an individual through the process in a simple process in order to get started easily, achieve positive outcomes, and keep making progress. Furthermore, these steps are designed to help an individual stay committed as well as motivated to make mindfulness meditation a part of his life.

There are three parts that make up the set of steps to mindfulness meditation. These include choosing an environment, beginning the meditation, and practicing mindfulness techniques.

Part 1: Choosing an Environment

Picking a Location

This involves think of a place where there is no distraction or interruption. The place does not need to be similar to Buddhist temple altar. In fact, you can choose a part of your home or even just by a tree outside. What is important is that the place feels peaceful and would allow you to detach from the circumstances of your daily life.

If you plan to foster mindfulness meditation, it is advisable to establish a space, which is only intended for meditation. You can put calming or inspirational items such as candles to soften the lighting, pictures of beautiful places, or fresh flowers.

Be Comfortable

Given that meditation requires being stationary for a certain period, you need to be comfortable. You have to make sure that the temperature in your chosen location or place to meditate suits your preference. It is advisable to have a blanket handy in case your body temperature drops. You can also make use of cushions or pillows to make you comfortable while sitting. It is also important that you wear comfortable clothes, which would not distract or bother you.

Allot Time

As you commit yourself to mindfulness meditation, it is important that you allot time for it. Initially, you may spend just 5 or 10 minutes in meditation. You may lengthen the time once you become comfortable with the practice. It is advisable not to begin your meditation for an hour or so to avoid being overwhelmed. You may start with small increments of time to allow yourself to fully commit to the practice. You may also set a timer to avoid getting tempted to check on the time while meditating. However, when the timer sets off, make sure it is gentle instead of a jolting alarm. It is suggested to look for a timer that has a soothing sound as that of a piano or chimes.

Trying Out the Postures

More often than not, people think of sitting with legs crossed or in lotus position when they encounter the term, "meditation." However, there are other positions in which you can meditation. The traditional position is sitting in a chair or on the floor; but, you can also stand, walk, or lie down. You can play around with these positions with or without pillows or cushions until you find out what feels the most comfortable to you. Remember, there is not "wrong" position to meditate. Take note that if you choose to lie down, avoid falling asleep. Most people are inclined to start a meditation and eventually fall asleep in the middle of the session. More information about the different meditation postures will be discussed in the last section of this chapter.

Part 2: Starting the Meditation

Settle Your Mind

This step takes a little time given that it is difficult to settle down and detach yourself from the things transpiring in your life. You may find that your mind is preoccupied with things that happened throughout the day or even about things that you think should happen in the future. It is more difficult to settle in after a stressful day as emotions begin to stir up. These circumstances are all right. You may find your mind dancing a bit and all you need to do is allow it to dance as you try to settle it. Take note that you might feel quite strange about meditation, especially if you are a beginner. All you need is to pause and take note of the feelings you are experiencing. You may eventually switch your focus to your physical position and make yourself comfortable.

Take Deep Breaths

This step involves bringing your awareness to your breath, taking note of the inhalations and exhalations of every breath. Then, feel how each breath works in your body. Feel the breath flowing in and out of the body, even as it fills your lungs and released through your throat and mouth. Then, try to deepen and lengthen every breath. As you take deep breaths, your mind and body becomes settled and relaxed. You can observe your breath for the entire duration of your meditation session. It should be noted that observing your breath is also a mindfulness technique.

Realize That You are Not What You Think

This step involves reminding yourself that you have control as to what thoughts or emotions you want to engage to. Remember that you are not your thoughts. Thus, you can release any thought or emotion that arises, specifically those that you do not wish to engage. Then, deviate your focus from such thought or emotion. By realizing that you have control over what you think and feel, you can change unpleasant thoughts and let go of them. Make sure you do not exert too much effort in taking note of your stream of thoughts. It takes a certain period of practice to be able to let go of mental occurrences without judgment.

Return to Your Breath

When you get distracted during mindfulness meditation, say, by thoughts, noises, or anything, make sure to go back to noticing your inhalations as well as exhalations. Return to focusing on your breath any time you encounter negative thoughts or emotions. When you are trying to focus on your breath, make sure that you focus on neutrality. For instance, if thoughts arise while you are focusing on your breath, maintain the practice of not judging your thoughts as well as how you are carrying out the meditation session. Once you allow yourself to judge your thoughts or emotions, your meditation session will be interfered. Remember, it is common for thoughts to arise or get distracted during meditation. Also, keep in mind that meditation is not a presentation; thus, it does not need to be error-free.

Focus on the Present Moment

As mentioned in previous sections, focusing on the present moment is one of the purposes of mindfulness meditation. While your mind and emotions are able to go back to the past or move forward to the future, your body still remains in the present moment. For this reason, many practices of mindfulness are body-driven. Thus, during meditation, if your mind wanders off, return to your body and focus on your breath. This will lead you to focus on the present moment alone.

Part 3: Practicing Mindfulness Techniques

Mindful Eating

Eating mindfully helps in losing weight as it calls for slowing down while you eat and enjoying your food as you taste it. Take for example eating an apple. You can practice mindful eating by holding the fruit and looking at it. Observe its form, texture, or anything present in its surface. Start feeling the apple either against your lips or in your hands. Bring the fruit closer to your face and try to smell it taking a few deep breaths. You might find your body responding by having the urge to eat the fruit or simply salivating. Then, take a bit of the fruit and observe its taste and texture. Notice if it is enjoyable to eat.

Mindful Walking

In the previous sections of this chapter, it was discussed that there are other positions to meditate apart from sitting.

Walking is one position that you can use while meditating. When you try to walk, notice the way it feels to walk, feeling your body move and your muscles bend and stretch. In order to focus on your movements more efficiently, slow down your pace. Feel your feet's sensation touching and leaving the surface you are walking on. When you choose to carry out a walking meditation, it is advisable to do so with barefoot. This helps heighten the experience. In addition, walking barefoot while meditating allows you to feel more sensations of your feet, including the temperature of the surface and its texture.

Focus on Sensations

If you feel pain or simply want to tune in to your body, it may help to carry out a sensation mindfulness meditation. Focusing on your sensations helps in decreasing tension and pain in your body. You may start by choosing a body part to focus on. You can opt for an internal or external body part. Once you have chosen the body part, notice if the sensations are neutral, pleasant, or unpleasant. You can take note if there is a feeling of pain, ache, or pleasantness in that particular body part. Observe how your mind as well as your body interacts with these feelings.

Make Everyday Chores a Meditation

So long as you do something mindfully, it can be a form of meditation. For instance, you can mindfully brush your teeth by feeling the toothbrush's bristles, tasting the toothpaste, and feeling the motion of your hand. You can also mindfully take a shower by take note of how you take care of your body during your bath. You can also do mindful driving as a meditation by observing how your body adapts to the seat, how you feel inside the care, and take note of the thoughts and emotions that arise when you are stuck in traffic.

As you do a mindfulness meditation, the most integral factor is to be in the present moment. Make sure to return to your breath and notice your thoughts and emotions without judging or following them.

During mindfulness meditation, it may help listening to soothing sounds or music, especially if you are just a beginner in the practice. In addition, do not rush things. Take the art of mindfulness meditation one step at a time. If you try to become aware of too many things, it can distract your meditation. You can only improve the amount of your awareness once you practice regularly. Finally, you can use a combination of postures to carry out a mindfulness meditation. It is advisable to try to experience all postures to find out what best suits your preference.

Other Mindfulness Meditation Postures

If you are unsuccessful in meditating while sitting on a chair or on the floor, you can try other meditation postures, including walking, standing, and lying positions.

Walking Mindfulness Meditation

Walking mindfulness meditation involves a transition between keeping your mind as still as your body and keeping your mind still in the middle of your activities. Walking in a meditative way allows you to practice the stillness of your mind while your body moves or acts. At the same time, it allows you to deal with minimal external disturbances.

The best time to practice meditating while walking is right after you have carried out a sitting meditation. Given that your mind is already still, it will be easier for you to do the walking meditation. However, some people find it easier and faster to settle down the mind while sitting rather than walking. This may be caused by trying the walking meditation first and then switching to sitting meditation. Nevertheless, it all depends on what you prefer.

If you have scheduled your meditation right after having dinner, it is advisable to carry out the meditation. This can help your body in digesting the food faster and prevent the feeling of sleepiness or drowsiness.

You can practice the walking meditation in two ways. One is walking back and forth on a straight, continuous path and two, going out for a stroll in the park or somewhere with minimal distractions. Walking back and forth on a straight path is more preferred by many individuals than going out for a stroll. However, for those who have no access to a quiet path, going out for a stroll is more convenient.

When walking back and forth on a straight, continuous path or a set path, the first thing to do is to choose a level path, preferably about 20 to 60 paces long. While a straight path is more conducive, you can also use an L-shaped or a U-shaped path. If you wish to set a timer during your meditation, make sure the timer is near your walking path. On the other hand, the timer should face away from your walking path to avoid getting tempted to look at it while meditating.

Once you have chosen your walking path, stand at one of its end for a while, clasping your hands together and placing them in front of you or even behind you. You should ensure that your arms hang down comfortably while clasping your hands. If you opt to place your hands in front, your palms should face your body. If your hands are behind you, your palms should face away from your body.

Then, close your eyes and take note if your body feels balanced. If you feel that your body leans to your right or left side, try to relax the muscles. The muscles are likely to cause the imbalance of your body.

Next, focus your attention to your breath by taking a couple of long, deep in-and-out breaths. Observe the sensations of the breath in one part of your body. Usually, most people who meditate choose a point on a line downwards the middle of their torso.

Open your eyes and look ahead of you. You can also choose to look down your walking path. On the other hand, make sure you avoid tilting your head forward. It is important to keep your head straight so you will stay aware of your inner focus on your breath. Start walking down the path at a normal pace. You can also opt to walk slightly slower; however, avoid glancing or gazing around as you walk down the path. Make sure to remain in your inner focus as you walk. In addition, make sure your breathing has a comfortable rhythm.

When you reach the other end of your walking path, pause for a moment and make sure your focus is still on your chosen point. If you notice that your mind has wandered off, focus on your breath again and face the opposite direction. Walk back to the end where you started your meditation, making sure your inner focus is on your chosen point.

On the other hand, when going out for a stroll, you have to create several rules for yourself so that you would not make it as just a regular walk. Choose an area, which is quiet. It is advisable to choose a place where it is less likely to be full of people. The area should have the slightest possibility of meeting someone you know and conversing with them. You can choose a back country lane or a quiet park.

In the event that you are just around your neighborhood, go to the direction that you do not usually take and where neighbors would not engage you in a conversation. If someone calls your name while walking, you may simply smile and nod without even speaking. If it is unavoidable to speak, simple answer back without saying anything unnecessary. Then, do the same techniques as that of walking in a straight path.

Standing Mindfulness Meditation

You might think that standing meditation is just a part of the walking meditation. It is more than just being a part of the walking meditation. Standing mindfulness meditation is useful for five conditions as you do the walking meditation.

For instance, when your mind wanders off, you simply need to pause and stand for a moment until you are prepared to reestablish your focus. Resume walking once you have regained focus. If your mind is restless, remain standing for a short period, making sure that your eyes are closed and your body is balanced or aligned. If you find yourself slouching, make sure to straighten up at once, pulling in your stomach and pulling back your shoulders down. This will create an arch in your back. If you notice that your body is leaning towards your right or left side, relax your muscles.

Another condition in which standing meditation is useful is when you get tired of walking meditation, yet you are not ready to stop your meditation. Remain standing for a few minutes while resting. However, make sure that your focus is in your posture.

Standing meditation allows you to spread awareness from one part of your body to another easier than other postures. Remain standing for several minutes as you engage in a comfortable breath. Then, allow your body to relax, making sure that your focus is on your whole body. Continue walking when you find that your awareness is already spread out to all your body parts.

When your mind has strong concentration in spite of the movement of your body, stop and remain standing. Meanwhile, when your mind encounters an interesting insight while walking, stop and remain standing for a few minutes and observe your mind. Make sure to avoid focusing on your posture. As you stand, your hands should be clasped together either in front or behind you just like in the walking meditation.

Lying Down Mindfulness Meditation

It is ideal to do the lying down mindfulness meditation if you want to develop a strong skill of concentration. More often than not, meditators find it more conducive to focus while lying down than carrying out a sitting meditation. There are also meditators who find lying down meditation difficult when it comes to developing a strong skill of concentration given that it is more conducive for sleeping.

As a general rule, it is best to lie down on your right side, on your back, or on your stomach but not on your left side. You can shift your position once you get tired of doing one posture. People who are sick prefer the meditation of lying down given that they are not able to endure sitting, walking, or standing.

Chapter 18: Mindfulness For A Happier Life

The saying goes: "you are what you think about." In our busy lives, we constantly have our heads full of thoughts about the future or about the past – it's usually thoughts about what we need to accomplish for that day, negative self-talk about past experiences or worrying thoughts about the future. This often means that we are never really living in the present moment. The majority of us walk around on 'autopilot' and never really immerse ourselves in the present moment.

This often means that we are just doing things out of unconscious habit, rather than clear and conscious decision. Practicing mindfulness meditation or other forms of mindfulness practices, will help bring a sense of calm and inner peace from our chaotic thoughts. It's so important to realise that life is only happening in the present moment – there is no future and there is no past. Thoughts about the future and past, are just constructs of the mind, because we can only experience life in the present moment.

When you truly realise this, it will liberate you.

It's one thing to know something, but when you fully embody it and integrate it into your lifestyle, then that's when conscious change and progression occurs. We all know that junk and processed foods are bad for us, but most of us still eat these kinds of foods. So there needs to be action, because words are just words without action. It really is that simple. Realise that life is happening right now. Not in the future or past, it's always in the present moment. Practicing mindfulness allows us to live life and prevent ourselves from being the victim of our minds. We can sit back and see our thoughts without judgment, personal identification or emotional response.

That's really why mindfulness creates a greater quality of life. It's so empowering and humbling to realise that our thoughts and perception create our reality. Most of us are victims of our own minds and we don't even realise it. It has been estimated that the average human being has 50,000 thoughts per day. These thoughts can either be positive and uplifting or negative and self-depleting. These thoughts literally shape our beliefs. If you harbour mostly negative thoughts, then those 50,000 thoughts will shape you to become a lot more pessimistic and self-destructive.

Mindfulness allows us to be, in a way, 'detached' from thoughts and feelings. Instead of being personally identified with our thoughts, we can see it in a more passive manner. Like we are a spectator rather than a victim. This brings great empowerment because you realise that you control your mind, rather than your mind controlling you.

You may also find that as you practice mindfulness more and more, your quality of life is enhanced and you feel a greater sense of gratitude and humility. The more you practice mindfulness, the more you will actually see how precious life is and how it is a beautiful gift. All we ever have is right now, life is not happening in any other time for us, only right now. It just goes to show how precious life is. You may have grand dreams of where you want to go, what you want to achieve or who you want to become, but if you can't fully appreciate right now, then even when you achieve great things, it will feel just as empty.

Chapter 19: Becoming Non-Attached

There's not a single good thing that comes out of developing attachments and if there's one, it is short-lived, as the negative side of attachments grows into us. Getting attached to someone or to something takes away your power, and more often than not, it ends up in a nasty experience. Let's say you are a young sweet woman with a bright future ahead. A prince charming comes along and sweeps your feet away. You are in love. Your world starts revolving around prince charming. It doesn't feel right when you go for a day without talking to them. When your prince charming is mad, you get mad, and when they are happy, you are happy too. It seems that your happiness is tied to their happiness. Then prince charming notices that you consider him to be a god among mortals. He starts despising you and his meager attempts to pull away inspires you to love him even harder. It is the sad classic tale of being attached to a person and it almost always ends in tears.

If you have been struggling with the negative habit of developing attachments, it's not easy to drop this habit. But there are mental training programs that would help us overcome this challenge. Mindfulness is one of the foolproof training that helps us to get rid of attachments and also equips us with a mindset that discourages getting attached in the first place.

The following are some of the ways that mindfulness allows us to fight against attachments.

No more getting wrapped up in fantasies

Nothing encourages us to get attached to something or to someone faster than a fantasy. When someone or something catches our fancy, we are quick to elevate them into a state of infallibility and what follows are vivid fantasies of what that person is like or how it would be so great to possess something. These fantasies hinder us from calling on the powers of our rational mind, and for that reason, we develop an attachment. Mindfulness empowers us to bring our focus to reality. Thus, our fantasies are banished away and now we have the mental clarity to see our situation for what it really is. The more we are able to think in a realistic way, the more we will behave in a well-adjusted manner, but if we are hanging on some fantasy, we are likely to exhibit strange behaviors.

Meeting your friends

Think about a young woman who has developed an unhealthy attachment to her boyfriend. She wants to spend all of her time with him and it doesn't matter whether he hurts her or not. She's blinded by her "love" for him. It would do such a woman a world of good if she tried to meet her friends. This is because our friends can be able to look at our situation through the lens of objectivity. Our friends can spot the inconsistency in our thinking and call us out on it. Furthermore, spending more time with your friends makes you realize that there are other important things needing your time besides your object of attachment.

Notice the disadvantages

It is not something that immediately occurs to us when we develop an attachment to something or someone. But noting down the disadvantages of this new development might awaken you from your negative habit. For instance, if you become attached to your spouse, so much that your whole days are spent thinking about them, they may have robbed you of time to check on your parents, do homework, and meet your clients. Ultimately, you will have to decide whether you can cope with these disadvantages.

Is this what we really want?

Call it desperation or what you may, but some of our behaviors are deeply unsettling. We could develop attachments as a way of coping with our inner battles and stay unaware. For instance, if we have been lonely for so long, we might become depressed about it. The next time we find a suitor or the next time someone shows interest in us, we will leap at them and plant our claws around them and declare them to be ours, never to let them go. The desperation can cause us to leap at virtually anything that moves. But in order to overcome this negative, we ought to ask ourselves whether what we have become attached to is something that we truly fancy. Taking a second hard look might jolt you awake from your crazy behavior.

Have a sense of fun

Instead of pursuing something and attaching yourself to it like glue, here's an approach that works. Have fun with it. Yes, you will spend time with the object of your interest, but the motivation will be different. You won't be looking upon this thing as the savior of your life, but you will be interested in knowing a little more about it. For instance, if you meet someone who is an absolute stunner, don't get their number and start text-bombing them with your declarations of your love for them. It's an obvious indication that you are fast getting attached, but even more than that, you pass off as creepy. Unless they are unstable too but expect that person to puff up their protective wings and try to distance themselves from you. But if you had approached them not as a needy person but as just a friend who's interested in knowing more about them, you will cover a lot more ground. They would let you into their life more easily. And getting to know what kind of person they truly are would probably kill the fantasy going on inside your mind and make you normal again.

Heal

The great thing about humans is that we have the capacity to know what's ailing us. If we are suffering from unhealthy attachments, we can certainly research it and understand our problem. What remains is to take action so that we are no longer held prisoners of our negative habits. With enough commitment, we should get started and complete the journey to full recovery.

Chapter 20: Decide Which Practice Is Right For You Today

Which of these forms of mindfulness described so far is most attractive to you? Plain and simple, **the practice that is right for you is the one you stick with**. The only metric that really matters in mindfulness is regularity. Mindfulness is bigger than good and bad, right and wrong. Skill at listening or breathing or tasting is not about being better; it's about having used a practice enough that when we are well and when our brains freak out, we notice. When we notice instead of running away from our emotional ups and downs, we have options for how we live each moment.

At the University of Connecticut School of Medicine, Dr. Julian Ford studies therapies that help individuals who experience post-traumatic stress disorder (PTSD). What he's learned over four decades is that veterans, survivors of natural disaster and abuse, and those who experience violence are capable of changing their brains from a constant alarm state to healthy functioning. Where before they had nightmares, outbursts of rage and constant anxiety, their alarms turn down when they focus on one thing at a time

But before you can focus, your brain needs you to be. Ford describes that moment as 'stepping back.' It's an ironic metaphor; we have have to step back and pause to truly be in control of our lives. It's not doing more and raising the intensity that give us more command of what thoughts occupy our minds and what emotions we feel. It is the mindful moment that leads to being able to truly choose and experience what we want and need.

As popular as mindfulness is becoming this is still the under-recognized, precious, , dumbfounding truth: the more mindful you are, the more whatever you want is possible. Once you are mindful, you are in control of what you decide to keep in your mind. Whatever you want can be the one center of your attention in that moment.

But, the research also reveals you have to practice before you need it. As with most stress management interventions, when you're already freaking out, it's hard to learn how not to freak out.

And what's crazy about our brains is that when we really start paying attention to stress or practicing mindfulness, we suddenly feel all the stress; we notice the tornado of thoughts we've been sublimating.

Thankfully, you can wait out the surge. Addiction recovery specialists teach that urges rarely last more than thirty minutes. This means that the painful thoughts or emotions that drive us to fix our minds or uncomfortable feelings with too much chocolate or wine can instead be approached with mindfulness.

To begin your practice, pick the technique you want to use consistently.

Chapter 21: What Is Mindfulness?

Mindfulness is the mindfulness that emerges when we purposely direct our consideration toward our internal experience, toward others, and the earth around us. Be that as it may, something beyond centering your mind, it's about your mindset—how you see the world. Mindfulness fortifies a mindset of being open, responsive, tolerating, and caring. And that starts with understanding your average propensity to pass judgment, expect you know something, or oppose what life brings or what is out of your control—things that everybody does. As you practice mindfulness, you'll begin to see shifts: from being on autopilot, occupied, uneasy, stressed over the past or future, to being alert, open, and tuned into the present; from being responsive in difficult minutes to having the option to calmly inhale and react with serenity and elegance; from being somewhere out in dreamland and making a decision about how things and individuals ought to be to considering something to be they are with bright, open neighborliness. You put down your ruler and learn acknowledgment and capable activity.

Your Evolutionary Biology in a Modern World

It may be to acknowledge; your mind is absent with what you are accomplishing for about portion of your life, 47 per cent of the time, by and large, agreeing to this fact. Is your mind not in the present? Then where will it be? Frequently,

We are ruminating, stressing, fixating,

judging, or busy with things that have just occurred or may occur: the develops of our mind, instead of reality. More often than not, you don't remain concentrated on the book you're perusing, the music you're tuning in to, or the associate who's addressing you. We mainly try not to remain present for substantial or terrible feelings like outrage and trouble. Might it intend to tip the scale the other way? Consider the possibility that you could be available for even 10 per cent a more significant amount of your life?

By creating mindfulness, you recover the minutes in your life by seeing and encountering them with complete consideration. You build up a method for being that is clear, sympathetic, and astute. It's an honest thought, yet a significant try in the present condition.

Your mind and sensory system, similar to all of you, are beautifully intended to keep you alive. Since you are worked for endurance, your mind's caution system is examining for dangers and setting off the "flight-battle solidify" stress reaction to escape what you decipher as a threat. Here and there, the perils are genuine; however, nowadays, we get activated for the day by a remark, a shock choice, an angry book, and likewise by how we identify with our obligations and to the individuals around us. As a human, your neurobiology is intended to respond rapidly instead of to react astutely; to feel pressure as opposed to adjusting; and to hear your internal pundit as opposed to positive, empowering expressions of plausibility. Besides, for security, you are worked to oppose the new and to separation yourself from the individuals who don't appear to be like you—at the end of the day, individuals who aren't in your clan. This propensity impedes joining and cooperation, also world harmony.

Take these attributes of our transformative science—we have minds that are wandering, examining, and getting occupied—and then outfit us with cell phones, PCs, and the Internet. The impacts are magnified. And to entangle our tech-soaked scene, we are associated like never before in a world that is unstable, unsure, complex, and equivocal (alluded to as VUCA), and it is straightforward the powers that met up to make what Time magazine initiated the "mindfulness unrest." Mindfulness brings shrewdness from the past to give a solution for now. That implies you can prepare your mind and body to enhance your experience even in this cutting edge world.

Being Human

Exploring the intricate world isn't all that mindfulness addresses, it likewise makes a difference
with the unavoidable difficulties that life brings, both the delight and the torment. Regardless of whether you're beginning to look all starry eyed at or accepting terrible news at
work, lamenting a misfortune or feeling overpowered by the enduring on the planet, you have
options both in how you identify with the experience and by the way you react. Mindfulness
causes you to become increasingly aware of your motivations in those minutes. Frequently when
times are hard (and here and there when bliss is extreme), our natural reaction is to

turn away from the distress and move in the direction of an outer departure to take the edge off: maybe it's TV, pharmaceuticals, shopping, online life, or a jug of wine. Even though you may get help, it's just brief. The more intelligent reaction is to bring thoughtfulness regarding what is difficult, and you can do this with mindfulness. Our opportunity and joy are in our capacity to pick how to appear for the correct life at this very moment.

The Science of Mindfulness

These are aptitudes that can be fortified and expanded. Research has indicated that you can change your default mental examples through rehashed practice, an idea called neuroplasticity.

The repetition of mental preparing, as a result, revamps your mind with new neural pathways that slope you to react to circumstances in more dexterous manners than naturally responding without much forethought. You get to be in the driver's seat of forming your cerebrum through intentional practice, rather than accidentally wiring your mind through the impact of social standards and your old propensities. Individuals frequently get some information about the difference between mindfulness and contemplation.

The two are particular, yet firmly associated: You can be mindful without Contemplating, yet the exploration shows that mindfulness reflection is the surefire approach to getting progressively mindful. Consider it like this: Meditation is to mindfulness as sports is to wellness. Contemplation is a body of mental preparing activities, and there are numerous structures, that are intended to create aptitudes, reinforce your mind, and produce quick states and long haul results.

Research on the advantages of contemplation has detonated as of late, and Richard. Davidson and Daniel Goleman propose that these mindful states begin to have enduring impacts. For instance, the customary empathy practice of "wishing well" not just makes a more prominent feeling of positive feeling and prosperity promptly in the meditator, yet additionally adds to progressively kind, liberal, and benevolent practices. In an ongoing meta-examination of the abundance of mindfulness Inquire about accessible, scientists found that mindfulness contemplation—keeping up a minute-by-minute open consciousness of our musings, sentiments, real sensations, and encompassing condition, frequently utilizing an object of center—increments attentional control, passionate guideline, and mindfulness. One research found that meditators lose less dark issue after some time contrasted and non-meditators; another investigation recommends that contemplation may diminish the psychological decrease related to maturing. Consideration has been appeared to change quality articulation, bringing down the body's provocative reaction to infection and other stressors, and to stretch telomeres, markers for the life span of life. Notwithstanding the overflowing of scientific research, stories from meditators around the globe confirm the advantages of predictable mindfulness practice. Mindfulness works

out, which you'll learn in numerous structures in the pages that pursue, can assist you with remaining wakeful and present, and tap into the forces of acknowledgment, appreciation, and sympathy. My understudies frequently disclose to me that they feel more opportunity in their day by day lives, just as more vitality and a more profound feeling of prosperity when they practice mindfulness—
regardless of whether using reflection or by doing regular exercises mindfully. As they increase more noteworthy knowledge into how their minds work and create more grounded mental skills, they feel progressively fit for settling on significant decisions, and they gain certainty from realizing that they can get to a quiet, grounded nearness on demand.

Here's the primary concern—and the unimaginable chance: You can figure out how to profoundly shift how you identify with your day by day encounters and to others. The mindfulness that emerges from mindful thoughtfulness regarding your internal musings, feelings, and discernments starts to bring a progressively striking point of interest for knowing yourself. This mindfulness is at the core of self-authority—of being the individual you need to be. It adds up to having a more extended, more extravagant life since you are available for a much a more significant amount of it. And we would all be able. The most effective method to Increase Your Mind Every Day If you've been enclosed in a room while a choral gathering is going on, observed kids playing out a school play, strolled along a stream in the woods, held the hand of somebody close to death, or investigated the substance of an infant, you know what the vitality of unadulterated nearness and association feels like.

Regular mindfulness is tied in with developing these distinctive minutes all the more reliably into your life—to discover satisfaction and marvel in common as opposed to sitting tight for exceptional events. Merely understanding that mindfulness is a trainable ability is an initial step, and now you have to realize how to go about it.

A significant number of us are accustomed to driving ourselves hard and might consider preparing an approach to attempt to constrain change, push, force, and weight ourselves into turning out to be something else. Mindfulness supports a different methodology. In this book, you will discover two fundamental methods for preparing: with formal, committed practices, regularly as a contemplation. You will likewise find unexpected ways of making that you incorporate into your day. In any case, the focal expertise is engaged thoughtfulness regarding

your body, contemplations, feelings, or surroundings at whatever point you notice that you're lost in thought. Consideration without anyone else's input might be centered. Yet, it becomes

mindfulness as it were at the point when combined with the aptitude of meta-mindfulness, the capacity to know your current perspective that screens that mindfulness. And there's another measurement to this: Mindfulness is tied in with focusing with thoughtfulness and sympathy, rather than judging or self-derided

Characteristics of Mindfulness

The accompanying ten characteristics do not just guide you toward mindful living; they can become some portion of what your identity is and how you see the world. Consider them frames of Mind, standards, and even mindsets that help and fortify mindfulness. Mindfulness isn't just about focusing; it additionally incorporates how you pay consideration. As you become acquainted with these mentalities, and practice and reinforce them with the contemplations and through the regular activities in this book, they will start to emerge as you become progressively mindful:

☐ Awareness emerges when you are alarm

and alert to whatever is in the minute-to-minute progression of your prompt understanding. It's the capacity to know, sense, see, feel, or to be mindful of what's going on, which is likewise called awareness. Aware mindfulness is the acknowledgment of what is available at this very moment, without judgment. At the point when you are available, you are mindful.

☐Beginner's Mind is considering things to be if just because, with receptiveness, receptivity, and interest. It's a reasonable focal point through which you suspend what you "know" about an item, individual, or idea, and enable yourself to look Outward (or internal) with more prominent lucidity. Apprentice's Mind is something contrary to being the master, and prepares for new thoughts, oddities, and results. Seeing with open-minded perspectives can bring back a feeling of miracle and wonder to individuals, circumstances, and minutes that have gotten common—which at that point welcomes appreciation and euphoria. ☐Acceptance is the limit and ability to consider things to be they genuinely are. We may not always like what we find—however, permitting sentiments and conditions to be, instead of attempting to oppose or attempting to drive change (which just makes battle and stress), is a decent start. A significant requirement here: Approval has nothing to do with being dormant. It's a functioning decision in which you figure out how to state, "This is the thing that life resembles at present," or my shorthand expression "It resembles this," without wishing things were different. **Acknowledgment makes way for giving up.**

☐ Insight is the moment of clarity of clearness. It's the ability to have a reasonable, exact understanding. It originates from trying different things with mindfulness and taking a gander at your contemplations, practices, and propensities. Mindful mindfulness encourages you to see circumstances and logical results in all that you do and causes you to create knowledge about how things work.

☐ Impermanence reminds us that nothing remains for what it's worth—in nature, climate, our bodies, feelings, political frameworks, and relational intricacies. However, we frequently wish things would stay the equivalent. At the point when you consider them to be as fleeting, you extend consideration regarding what is here now since you welcome that it is transitory. And you endure less when things do change, realizing that you were entirely present for the interface, appreciate, and make the most of your life as it was and is in every minute.

☐Serenity is the condition of passionate tranquility or no reactivity; it is being mindful of anything that is occurring without being cleared away by it—great or terrible. This frame of Mind includes figuring out how to set aside your inclinations so that you can be with what's there. There are a ground-breaking opportunity and an unavoidable, easygoingness to poise. At the point when you develop

serenity, life's everyday issues won't shake you
and overpower you to such an extent, and you won't want to stick to what's pleasurable.

It's identified with tolerance, which is the capacity to keep up self-restraint notwithstanding things you don't like or to stay with stressful circumstances in any event,
when they don't resolve as rapidly as you'd like.

☐ Interconnection is the nature of the world we live in, and it can turn into the nature of
ourselves, as well. Thich Nhat Hanh urges us to see interfering with others, with nature,
with the whole worldwide environment. This state of Mind impacts how we care for each
other: We perceive that we are reliant on one another, and are mindful of how we influence our territory and everyone

around us. We are ourselves, and yet we are on the whole each other, individuals with fears, trusts, and the aching for adoration. ☐ Compassion is taking care of the experience of enduring with the desire to ease it. It's applied in the longing to lessen the enduring of others or decrease our misery (self sympathy). Sympathy begins with compassion—understanding and being delicate to the experience of torment or uneasiness—and adds the segment of trying to be of administration, to bring some level of alleviation. There is liberality in empathy. You can inquire yourself, what might best serve here?

☐Gratitude originates from focusing on what is excellent, with gratefulness for it. There are two segments to being thankful. The first is avowing that there are beneficial things on the planet and that you get gifts and benefits. The second is perceiving that the wellsprings of these great things are outside of you. Others—or if you're of an otherworldly mindset, a higher power—add to the positive pieces of your life. This strengthens that you're a piece of an option that is greater than yourself, and advances sentiments of having a place, interconnection, and delight. Gratitude produces the feeling of "I have enough," a springboard for liberality.

Bliss is a profound feeling of prosperity imbued with enchant. Satisfaction is an intrinsic human limit, associated with your capacity to encounter marvel and wonderment. It originates from inside, not from external conditions, individuals, or prizes.

Mindfulness causes you to perceive what brings you euphoria and what squares it. And it encourages you to discover approaches to get to this uplifting quality in regular day to day existence.

Mental Training Basics

We realize that whatever your practice becomes more grounded: For instance, each time you discover your Mind wandering and then divert your consideration, you fortify your meta mindfulness. Consider it a "mental rep," simply like the activities you may do at the rec center or the drills on the piano. Coming up next are a lot of center practice that train the central skills and mentalities of mindfulness and empathy. What pursues are the nuts and bolts—and all through the book, you will find specific applications and approaches to weave these, alongside extra practices, into your day.

Mindful Breathing

Following your breath, as you breathe in and breathe out is the fundamental mindfulness reflection practice that trains consideration, develops mindfulness, settles the Mind, and quiets the body. The breath fills in as a grapple for consideration that you can utilize any place you are. At the point when your Mind wanders, you return it to your grapple and reinforce your capacity to coordinate, balance out, and continue your concentration voluntarily. You will find out about different stays you can utilize later in the book—yet recollect that the breath is always accessible to you. The accompanying advances are a dependable, characteristic approach to quiet yourself

and return to the present:
1. Feel the vibes of breathing: air coming in at the nose, and your chest or stomach area rising and falling. 2. Perceive when your mind wanders, and tenderly return your thoughtfulness regarding the breath.

3. Pursue the full cycle of breathing: the breath in, then blow out, and space in between breaths.

4. Utilize accommodating expressions, for example, In, Out, or Here Body Scan Regularly educated as to the primary conventional practice for amateurs, the body check is an approach to deliberately moving consideration through your body, each part in turn. The best method to reinforce mindfulness is to carry mindfulness to the body, where you begin to grow high-goals consciousness of feelings. The vast majority are detached from the body,

yet as you practice the body examine, you show signs of improvement at recognizing feelings by perceiving the physiological vibes that give ascend to them. Feelings start in the body—for instance, a held stomach might flag dread. Feelings are physical reactions to upgrades—regardless of whether they are somebody's radiating grin, an unexpected vehicle horn, or an unexpected telephone call. As you become increasingly acquainted with occupying your body, it turns into a rich wellspring of information that can illuminate and control choices. You can do a body check in a couple of minutes, or in 30. I suggest beginning with around 10 minutes.
1. Start in a place that is alert and loose. Enable your eyes to close tenderly if you like. Feel the

full help of the floor or the seat underneath your body. 2. Start with relaxing. Enable your breath to stream regularly, effectively streaming in and out of your body. If you become diverted or your mind wanders duringthe body examines, you can take your consideration back to your breath, and then pick up the last known point of interest. 3. The first spotlight on your lower body. On your next breath out, pursue that breath all the path down through your body and focus on your feet. Beginning with left or right, notice any vibes of shivering, temperature, or beating. Go attention to your toes, the bundle of your foot, the impact point, the curve, the top of your foot. At that point, climb to the lower leg, lower leg, upper leg on the two sides, As you do as such, attempt to discharge vibes of snugness or strain.

4. Proceed with this procedure for your entire body up to your head. As you check in with each piece of your body, you may see solid sensations, for example, warmth or coolness, weight, or hurting. Check whether you can see without judging, assessing, or inciting your mind to wander off in a tale about what gave ascend to the sensation.

5. At long last, when you've moved from your toes to the crown of your head, be mindful of your body overall. Take a full breath that draws in your whole body, trailed by an unwinding breathe out. Carry a delicate grin to your face. Notice any physiological vibes that emerge because of grinning.

Conclusion

There is so much you can learn through mindfulness and its associated practices, and the benefits are endless when you genuinely apply yourself and your attitude to improve. We are so busy living our lives with what we now consider unavoidable distractions. It's easy to forget techniques still exist to regain control over the thoughts and emotions we allow to build ourselves up or cut us down. Acknowledging the basic need to create a safe space to assess and improve our self-awareness is critical in our self-development and in maintaining our professional and personal lifestyles. The beauty of mindfulness is that you carry it from one moment to the next, and this evolves to become a continuous chain throughout the course of your life. It can be there whenever and wherever you need it, guiding you to a positive outcome in the face of challenging or difficult situations.

The most important element you can leave behind after reading this book is unending judgement. Once you take that out of the equation, you allow yourself to recognize and accept the definition of 'you', and you become more compassionate with more to offer. Herein lies the law of attraction – when you become happier with who you are, you attract others of a similar mindset, but that's a whole other book!

If you've read this book but haven't had the chance to practice the exercises mentioned, I strongly suggest taking the time to try them out. If you're looking for additional reading, a great place to start without becoming overwhelmed are inspirational quotations (there are a number of great books, websites, and even phone apps). These quotations can really help to put you in the right frame of mind to face each day with equality and to change your priorities so that positivity is your main focus. By refocusing on positivity, you will discover inner strength and stamina you can use to overcome situations while allowing your mind to rest from being fed with constant negativity, and it will repay you a thousand times over. If you're looking for reading material more related to the spiritual side of mindfulness, Khalil Gibran is an excellent author that discusses the dilemmas of life from a spiritual stance. **The Prophet** is one such book that I would recommend as valuable reading to anyone seeking this path.

www.ingramcontent.com/pod-product-compliance
Lightning Source LLC
Chambersburg PA
CBHW072002070526
44583CB00015B/1300